The Names of History

The Names of History

On the Poetics of Knowledge

Jacques Rancière

Translated by Hassan Melehy

Foreword by Hayden White

University of Minnesota Press
Minneapolis
London

The University of Minnesota Press gratefully acknowledges translation assistance provided for this book by the French Ministry of Culture.

Originally published as *Les Noms de l'histoire*. © by Éditions du Seuil, Paris, 1992. Collection La Librairie du XXe Siècle sous la direction de Maurice Olender.

Published by the University of Minnesota Press
2037 University Avenue Southeast, Minneapolis, MN 55455–3092
Printed in the United States of America on acid-free paper

Library of Congress Cataloging-in-Publication Data
Rancière, Jacques.
    [Mots de l'histoire. English]
    The names of history : on the poetics of knowledge / Jacques Rancière ; translated by Hassan Melehy ; foreword by Hayden White.
        p.   cm.
    Includes bibliographical references and index.
    ISBN 0-8166-2401-1 (alk. paper). — ISBN 0-8166-2403-8 (pbk. : alk. paper)
    1. History—Philosophy. 2. Literature and history. 3. Historiography—France—History—20th century.   I. Title.
D16.8.R2713
901—dc20   94-7212

Contents

Foreword: Rancière's Revisionism

Hayden White

This long "essay" on the political, scientific, and literary status of historical discourse was originally developed for presentation in a lecture series
at Cornell University on "the politics of writing." In it Jacques Rancière is
concerned with the politics of historical study and writing, the ways in
which historians conceptualize, speak, write about, and in writing about,
effectively constitute in politically significant ways that "history" which
is, supposedly, their common object of study. In other words, this is not a
study of "history" understood as "the past" in which certain kinds of
events occurred—although it offers very strong views on the nature of this
"past." It is, rather, a meditation on "historical discourse," the ways in
which we speak about this past and the ways in which it speaks, fails to
speak, or is prohibited from speaking to us. The original title of Rancière's
book was *Les Mots de l'histoire* (The words of history). I have a copy of
the first edition, which I bought in Paris in November 1992, before me as I
write this foreword. But, I am informed, the title was changed in the second printing to *Les Noms de l'histoire*. That's too bad. I prefer the original
title, with its echoes not only of Sartre's autobiography (*Les Mots*) but also
of Foucault's great study of the modes of Western knowledge production
(*Les Mots et les choses*). By "les mots" Rancière designates all the
"words" that comprise the documentary evidence on which historians base

their accounts of the past and also all the "words" that have been written by historians in those accounts. What happens to the words *of* history when they are used as the raw materials for words *about* history? What ought we to do with history's words? What are our obligations to those words spoken in the past, only some of which find their way into the (official) record, but most of which are lost and can be recovered only with the most arduous labor? What are the historian's obligations to the words of the dead? Are these obligations more important than modern, social scientific historians' efforts to apply models of structure and laws of process to the past?

The Words and the Things of History

Rancière is interested, then, in the relationship between the "words of history" and the "things" of the past that they indicate, name, or otherwise signify, whether these be events, persons, structures, or processes. But he is also interested in the relationship between these "words" and the "things" of the past that they misname, unname, obscure, or otherwise ignore. This is why, in part, the study and writing of history must be considered, first and foremost, less as a scientific discipline than as a "discourse" in which history's *possible objects of study* are identified, various *methods or procedures for studying them* are debated, and *a proper manner of speaking* about such objects is contrived. The prosecution of this threefold discursive task is an exercise in what Rancière calls "the poetics of knowledge," where "poetics" is understood in the sense of a "making" or "invention" of a "discipline" for the study of the past that will be at once scientific, political, and literary.

But not scientific, political, and literary in either a general or a traditional sense. No, in Rancière's view, the modern study of history must be scientific in the sense of seeking to become a systematic search for the latent (what is hidden and indeed unseeable) in, below, or behind the phenomena that manifest the existence of "a past." So, farewell to the older *empiricist* ideal of historical investigation. History must construct its objects of study rather in the way that, in psychoanalysis, the unconscious has to be constructed as an object of study on the basis of its symptomatic effects or, in physics, electrons must be posited on the basis of the trails they leave in a bubble chamber, rather than by direct observation. History can no more feign finding its objects of study already formed and awaiting the eye of the impersonal observer than can psychoanalysis or physics.

For example, a historical personage such as Napoleon must be presumed to have existed and to have done certain things at certain times, things worthy of note and indeed actually noted in the historical record; but the words (or signs) "Napoleon" and "the life and career of Napoleon" name phenomena that are as much effects of causes more extensive or symptoms of structures more basic than any merely "factual" account of Napoleon's "life" could even begin to indicate. Most important, according to Rancière, lying beneath or behind or within that "career" are the lives, thoughts, deeds, and *words* of the nameless millions of people who made that career possible, participated in it, were ruined or destroyed in the course of and because of it, and left their *anonymous* mark, their *unidentifiable* trace on the world of that time. The retrieval of the history of that nameless mass, including the "poor" who were more patients than agents of the Napoleonic moment of history—the return of these victims of history to their rightful place in history—is a duty, Rancière tells us, at once scientific *and* political. It is a scientific duty insofar as it restores to the domain of knowledge a body of fact lost through a negligence or enmity both scientific and political. And it is a political duty insofar as it contributes to the legitimation of the democratic program peculiar to the modern age by substantiating the claim of the anonymous masses and nameless poor to a place in history. Thus, Rancière takes up arms on behalf of Walter Benjamin's idea that the story of victors must be balanced, even supplanted, by the story of the vanquished, the abject, and the downcast of history.

History and Politics

Like a number of other philosophers—Hannah Arendt and Jean-Luc Nancy come to mind—Rancière suggests that participation in politics hinges on conceptions of membership in communities whose pedigrees are either confirmed or denied by an appeal to "history." But this "history" is a construction of those who already enjoy membership and indeed privileged positions in already formed communities. No appeal to "the facts" alone can touch this construction, because these same constituencies control what will count as the appropriate kind of science for determining, not only "what are the facts" but also and most important "what can count as a fact."

In the nineteenth and well into the twentieth century, "history" consisted of the doings of kings or of those states, social castes, or nations that had arrogated to themselves the equivalent of a royal authority. This kind of historiography often was based on what Rancière characterizes as "royal-empiricist" principles, in honor of its first theorist, Thomas Hobbes. The philosopher of order as against freedom, Hobbes equated the irresponsible use of words with civil disobedience and the circulation of stories about rebellious subjects with incitement to revolution. He was one of the first to recognize that civil unrest and rebellion could be fomented by the reading of those old histories that told of political dissidence, heresy, and tyrannicide in ancient times. "Royal-empiricist" historiography, deriving from a belief in the Hobbesian notion that responsible historiography would deal with the manifest content of history, the deeds of kings and states, became orthodoxy for the discipline of history established in the early nineteenth century. From then on, orthodox historians would limit themselves to telling only "what really happened" on the basis of what could be justified by appeal to the (official) "historical record." They would deal in proper language and tell proper stories about the proper actions of proper persons in the past. Thus, insofar as history could be called a science, it was a discipline of "propriety."

History and Science

Just after World War I, however, the *Annales* group, under the leadership of Lucien Febvre, began the process of transforming traditional, (political) event-oriented, "empirical," and storytelling historical studies into a discipline modeled on and utilizing the techniques of modern, structuralist, and statistical social sciences. This meant, among other things, probing beneath the evanescent, surface "froth" of political events, identifying the levels of social, economic, and ultimately natural (geographical, climatic, epidemiological, etc.) processes; assigning these levels relative importance as causal forces over the long term; and mapping the effects on one level to their conditions of possibility arising on another, more basic level by statistical correlations. Under the leadership of Fernand Braudel, the heirs of the *Annales* group succeeded in dominating historical studies, not only in France but over the whole of European culture. For a long while, the *Annalistes* were thought to have transformed history into a science, but Rancière is critical of this claim. In his view, the *Annales* group did little more than transform history into an appendix of the social sciences—and gutted it of its human content in the process.

History and Historians

Rancière's assessment of the achievement of the *Annales* group is a major element in his argument about the current condition and future tasks of historiography. What he argues is that they did succeed in undermining (though not by any means destroying) the older, event-oriented, story-telling kind of history writing. But, he concludes, in doing so they also succeeded in depriving history of its human subject, its links to a generally political and specifically democratic agenda, and its characteristic mode of representing its subject's manner of being in the world, namely, narrative.

Rancière's own mode of presenting what turns out to be an indictment of modern historical discourse warrants comment. His style is more lyrical than impersonal, more aphoristic, even oracular, than demonstrative or argumentative. While Rancière presumes a "story" of history's development as a discourse and a discipline, he does not fill out the details of this story, nor does he deal with any specific historical work in depth. Rather, he focuses on a few of the practices of a few historians (Braudel, Jules Michelet, E. P. Thompson, Alfred Cobban, François Furet, Pierre Chaunu, and others), each of whom is used as a representative of the strain of thought about history that Rancière invokes in order to help him make his case about what went wrong in modern historical thought and how it might be made better.

It is evident—from what Barthes would have called his "table of obsessions"—that Rancière writes from the perspective of the (French) political Left, but Marxist historians escape Rancière's indictment no less than the *Annalistes*. He regards the Marxist attention to the "masses" as a ruse by which to evade the difficult work of inscribing "the poor" within history's domain. Like the *Annalistes*, Marxist historians participated in an ornate obfuscation by which "history" was deprived at once of its "events," its human "subjects," and any possible "political" meaning.

History and Literature

Along with their distaste for the singular "event," the *Annalistes* also wanted finally to release history "from the indeterminacy of . . . words" and the "true-false" language of stories and endow it with the "language of truth." Rancière studies a number of the enigmas, paradoxes, and contradictions that mark the effort to fuse the language of stories with the imperatives of historical truth, and he tries to revise the conventional story of the effort to transform the study of history into a science. This is what he means by an exercise in the "poetics of knowledge," which he defines as "a study of the set of literary procedures by which a discourse escapes literature, gives itself the status of a science, and signifies this status." In other words, this is a study of a certain technique of writing by which a discourse originally belonging to "literature" escapes from this "literature" and, *by the use of literary techniques*, constitutes itself as a "science."

This argument should not be taken, Rancière insists, as an attempt to deny the difference between science and literature, reject the cognitive authority of science, or return history to the status of a "fictional" discourse. We must not forget, Rancière reminds us, that if the nineteenth century was the age of science and the age of history, it was also the age of "literature." By this, Ranciere means to stress that it was in the nineteenth century that "literature" named itself as such and distinguished itself from "the simple enchantments of fiction." Indeed, in the nineteenth century, "literature" laid claim to the status of a kind of knowledge every bit as "realistic," rigorous, and self-critical as either science or history. And this "literature" participates in that nineteenth-century effort to survey the "broad masses and great regularities" of history, and not only those that "lend themselves to the calculations of science" but also those that manifest "a new disorder and arbitrariness" that must disturb any effort to represent them in any of the forms provided by premodernist "fictional" writing.

History and the Masses

But the "broad masses" that manifest "a new disorder and arbitrariness"—
the disorder and arbitrariness of democracy—are not the object of study of
the new "science" of history. On the contrary, since science cannot handle
these "broad masses," history ends up in the paradoxical position of denying, not only that certain events were meaningful, but even that what are
most obviously the great events ever happened at all. Thus, for example,
Rancière points out, Alfred Cobban's *Social Interpretation of the French
Revolution* tends to the conclusion that "the Revolution didn't take place
or that it had no place to be." And François Furet's position comes down to
much the same thing, namely, that the Revolution was a result, not of any-
body's action, but rather of the fact that there was a "vacancy of power."
France in the late eighteenth century, Furet tells us, was a "society without
a state." Consequently, the Revolution took over an "empty space" by the
"'reign of democratic rhetoric' and domination of societies in the name of
the 'people'." That is to say, the Revolution defeats something that does
not exist, a nonentity: the Old Regime. It had ceased to exist long before
the outbreak of the Revolution; therefore, the revolutionaries were delud-
ed in thinking that there was something to rebel against. Modern "scientific" history shows us that there was nothing but a "vacancy" in that historical place supposedly occupied by the Old Regime. According to Rancière,
Furet essentially tries to demonstrate that "the Revolution is the illusion of
making the Revolution, born from ignorance of the Revolution already
being made." And Furet ends in the paradoxical position of asserting that
"something took place that had no place to take place."

   Ranciere's critique of modern, social scientific historical studies is radical: it goes to the very root of their political raison d'être. Originating in the
desire to serve the political interests of the modern state and based on the
documentary record produced by ambassadors, generals, and ministers of
these authorities, historians had originally stressed the reality and the primacy of the political event as history's basic unit of meaning. Historical
writing cast in the form of a narrative purported to be an impersonal
observer's objective observation of the events produced by these historical
actors and agencies. When, however, with the advent of the modern democratic social movements, the demand arose for a similarly objective

account of new collective and popular historical actors and agencies, it suddenly became inconvenient to dominant powers to have their stories told. Whence the rebellion among historians of both the Left and Right political persuasions against the "event" and against "storytelling." By denying the reality of events in general, one could deny the reality of an event such as the Revolution, the meaning of which was its status as a manifestation of the emergence of the anonymous masses of history, the poor, the abject, and the oppressed, onto the stage of history as actors in their own right. The significance of this event could be denied by denying the reality of events in general and thus the reality of the event that was supposed to have manifested it, the Revolution. The denial of the reality of the historical event was the real significance of the putative transformation of history into a "social science" by Marxists and *Annalistes*, on the one side, and by political conservatives such as Cobban and Furet, on the other. The rejection of narrative as the discursive mode for the representation of historical events followed for two reasons: first, there could be no "realistic" narratives without belief in "real events"; and, second, history could never become scientific until it transcended the delusory seductiveness of storytelling.

Thus, Rancière's scenario of the betrayal of history by the Left and the Right and by those who believed history should become a science as well as by those who believed it should remain an art. In the disappearance of the event, according to Rancière, "the scholarly pretension of history, taken to the limit where its object is eradicated, comes to extend its hand to the scholarly pretension of politics." "History" is now obscured by "historiography" and thereby makes itself ready for transformation into "a division of political science, . . . devoted to the study of the aberration that causes the event of speech to proliferate through the cracks of political legitimacy"— as, ironically, Hobbes had recommended three centuries earlier.

Michelet's Epistemological Break

History—in both senses of the term: the events and the account of the events—thus disappears into the dark hole of the modern social sciences, and the new subject of history—the masses—announced by the Revolution is repressed once again. This repression of the masses is signaled, in Rancière's view, by modern historians' ambivalence toward the founding figure of modern French historiography, Jules Michelet. On the one hand, everyone appears to honor Michelet as a great historian and above all a great writer, a master of French prose, the identifier of topics never before seriously studied by historians (such as "women," "witchcraft," "the sea"), and, in the case of the *Annalistes*, as the progenitor of their own brand of "scientific" historiography. On the other hand, he is regarded as a typical "Romantic," who sentimentally celebrated the spirit of the common people, idolized "France," deified "nature," and often degenerated into lacrimose effusions of "poetic" writing that had nothing to do with science. In a word, Michelet is both honored and vilified, celebrated and forgotten—exactly like the historical subject that he, more than any other, was responsible for identifying and bringing back to life: the People.

According to Rancière, the ambivalence shown toward Michelet is a result of the fact that he was the formulator of that threefold contract—scientific, political, and literary—that modern historical consciousness has succeeded in violating under the sign of history's scientization. In Rancière's view, Michelet was responsible for nothing less than "a revolution in the poetic structures of knowledge." It was his achievement to have "invented a republican-romantic paradigm of history" to oppose the "royal-empiricist" model. And it is this paradigm that remains necessary "as long as [history] wishes to remain . . . history and not a comparative sociology or the annex of economic or political science." The paradigm constituted by Michelet—often thought of as simply a version of "Romanticist" historiography—actually features new and utterly original concepts of the "subject" of history, the historical "event," and the kind of narration adequate to the representation of both this subject and this event in writing. The new subject of history is nothing other than all the persons and groups who died mute, unnoticed, and unheard but whose voices continue to haunt history with their repressed presence. The new historical "event" is presented as such personified or incarnated abstractions as "the poor," "women," "the Revolution," "France," and "the native land." Beyond that, Michelet develops a new way of dealing with the documentary record—all the words written down in such a way as to both reveal and conceal the speech of the forgotten ones of the past: this is Michelet's new science of historical research, in which the difference between what the document *says* and what it *signifies* is dissolved. Whereas both traditional historiography and the newer scientific variety had treated the event as something that could be known only by way of the document, as something represented but also displaced by the document that indexed its occurrence, in Michelet, Rancière asserts, "the document [becomes] identical to the event itself." Michelet goes into the archives not in order to *read* the documents as the dead indices of events now past, but in order to immerse himself in those documents *as* fragments of the past still living in the present. Instead of effecting the pose of impersonal observer of an objective reality, in Michelet the historian himself enters onto the stage of history, addresses the reader in his own voice, which, because it is itself a voice of the people, is nothing other than the voice of the documents themselves. Instead of interpreting the documents, Michelet lets them *speak* for themselves by *showing* them to us. The difference between the *dead written* word, which, like a corpse, can only be *viewed,* and the *live spoken* word, which can only be *heard*, is effaced. In this way Michelet invents a "new solution to the excess of words, . . . he invents *the art of making the poor speak by keeping them silent, or making them speak as silent people . . . the historian keeps them silent by making them visible*."

Thus does Michelet perform a revolution in writing by which "the narrative of the event becomes the narrative of its meaning." And he does this by "telling us not their content but the meaning of their content; telling us this meaning instead of producing it as the explication of the content of the narratives." In a word, Michelet, in dissolving the difference between the document and the event, also collapses the distinction between the form of the historian's text and its content. The historian's text is not only *about* history, it *is* history; its substance is continuous with what it speaks about.

Finally, Michelet invents an utterly new kind of narrative, what Rancière dubs "the narrative that is not one." Indeed, whereas older (and newer) historians consider the story (the events, the facts arranged in the order of their occurrence) to be one thing and their discourse (their arguments, explanations, or commentary) about the events that comprise the story to be quite another, Michelet collapses the distinction between the narrative and the discourse. Thus, he invents the "narrative-discourse" by eliminating the *opposition* between past tense and present tense and replacing it with the authority of the *present*, "so as to mark the immanence of meaning in the event." This is reflected in Michelet's perfection of the absolute nominal phrase, which "abolishes every temporal mark in order to absolutize . . . the meaning of the event." What, for example, is being expressed/represented/referred to in the passage in which Michelet, in the presence of the Festival of Unity of Summer 1790, writes: "No conventional symbol! All nature, all mind, all truth!"? Rancière's answer: "*All truth*, then, where the distinctions of tense, mode, and person disappear, the distinctions that place the truth in question by relativizing the event or the position of the narrator." Here, in the "the nominal phrase . . . is an essential poetic structure of the new historical knowledge. . . . The nominal phrase effaces [the] nontruth . . . uncertainty, death, inessentiality." The truth in question is that which hitherto *logos* (reason, discourse, science) had purported to liberate from the obscurities of *muthos* (myth, story, religion). Now, the very distinction between *logos* and *muthos* is effaced. The kind of truth in which Michelet dealt "signifies more than the exactitude of the facts and figures, the reliability of the sources, and the rigor of the inductions." His is the truth expressed in "the ontological modality to which a discourse is devoted."

Michelet as Modernist

The claims made for the originality of Michelet and the pertinence of his work to the understanding of the contemporary poetics of historical knowledge are extraordinary. Rancière presents Michelet as the model for what historical research should have become in order to live up to the terms of its threefold contract—scientific, political, and literary—with modern democratic political constituencies. By dismissing Michelet as a mere "romantic," a poet, and sentimental devotee of an idealized "people" or by praising him for having discovered a new "subject" of history (collectivities, mentalities, anonymous forces) but at the same time ignoring his "methods" (of research and writing), modern historians were able to continue the age-long tradition of keeping "the poor" in their place—outside of history—and of pretending to be relating nothing but facts—and ignoring their meanings. Actually, Rancière argues, Michelet augured the emergence, beyond both Marxism and the *Annalistes*, of a genuinely *modernist* science of history that might finally identify the true but repressed *subject of history*. Similarly, Michelet anticipated a distinctively modernist manner of writing alone capable of presenting history's true "subject" and putting this subject in its proper place "in history."

In such seemingly bizarre tropes as those in which he endows a natural phenomenon such as "mud" or a cultural practice such as the "harvest" with a "voice," Michelet appears to prefigure the kind of writing practiced by the Joyce of *Finnegans Wake* or Virginia Woolf or Proust, a manner of writing that effectively liberates "literature" from both "fiction" and "mimesis." "By making the mud or the harvests speak in place of the orators and writers of the people," Rancière says, Michelet "gives a common root to the reign of the people and their scholarly history in their proper place. He gives a body to this place so that the voice of this body will pacify their turmoil. He puts in place the subject of democracy and at the same time the object of science."

So, pace the social scientists, the Marxists, and the *Annalistes*, history does not become a science by ceasing to be "narrative" or "romantic" or "literary." On the contrary, Rancière suggests, it was romantic writing in the form of Michelet's antinarrative, antimimetic, and antiliteralism that made "literature" available to history as a "discourse of the truth."

The Unconscious of Historical Discourse

What is the status of Rancière's own discourse? I remarked earlier on the nonnarrative and nondiscursive, aphoristic, almost oracular nature of his text. In this respect, Rancière's own text resembles that of his "romantic" hero, Michelet, or his "modernist" models, Joyce, Woolf, and Proust. That is to say, it is impossible to distinguish between the literal and figurative levels of his discourse. And this makes it virtually impossible to submit what he asserts about anything whatsoever to any test of falsifiability on the basis of evidence. Like Michelet's "absolute nominal phrase," the meaning of Rancière's assertions is indistinguishable from their "being said." There is a sense in which Rancière wishes to play the "silent witness," the witness who, instead of speaking *about* history, *is* history. We can say of Rancière's discourse what he himself says of the age in which he lives:

> The democratic and social age is then neither the age of the masses nor that of individuals. It is the age of hazardous subjectification, engendered by the pure opening of the unlimited, and constituted

from places of speech that are not designatable localities but rather singular articulations between the order of speech and that of classifications.

Rancière himself launches his discourse from a "place of speech" that is not "a designatable locality," and this place is that of a "singular articulation" somewhere between "the order of speech" and the "order of classifications." What he has tried to do, as I see it, is place himself in the liminal zone between any given present and any possible past and try to resist the impulse to fall into the abyss between "speech" and "classification." This abyss is what Rancière sees as the problem to be confronted at the level of "the poetics of knowledge." His own speech is to be taken neither literally nor figuratively; his own mode of address is to be taken as neither active nor passive; and his assertions are to be taken as neither denotative nor connotative.

What Rancière has attempted—and it is a very original attempt—is to disclose "the unconscious" of historical discourse, everything that had to be repressed in order to make possible the specific kinds of historical discourse met with in our culture in our age. He has put himself in the difficult position of the speaker *for* history who does not know exactly what he is saying and why he is saying it. And all this in the interest of revealing the stakes, no less political than they are scientific and literary, in daring to think about "history" at all.

Throughout his text, Rancière speaks of the "revisionists," by which he means not only those who seek to deny that the Holocaust ever happened, but also all of those who seek, in the interests of the status quo, to deny that anything that might threaten the status quo could ever have happened at all. His own work, coming *after* the efforts of both Marxists and *Annalistes* to transform history into a science, wishes to revise those efforts in the sense of reconsidering where they went wrong and where they failed. But Rancière's own revision becomes less a revision of history than of science, politics, and literature all at once. Traditional historians will not understand this book. Scientific historians will reject it. But those historians who continue to honor history's links to "literature" will find much to admire in it and not a little to imitate.

Acknowledgments

This book began as a seminar held at the International College of Philosophy in 1987–88. Its first systematic presentation was proposed in the context of the Perroquet Conferences in May of 1989. An invitation from the Western Societies Program and the Department of History at Cornell University allowed me to continue the research through a series of lectures on the politics of writing in the fall of 1990. Finally, I would like to thank my friends at Duke, Santa Cruz, and Berkeley, who have read and responded to my work.

A Secular Battle

"For more than a century, those interested in history—and they are many—have struggled with the word."

Thus speaks one of the masters of the discipline. And his intention appears, at first sight, easy to understand. The historians who wished to break with the old tradition of chronicling, in order to give history, to the greatest extent possible, the rigor of a science, had to struggle with the presuppositions and equivocations attached to the very name of history. A history, in the ordinary sense, is a series of events that happen to subjects who are generally designated by proper names. Now, the revolution in historical science has precisely aimed to abolish the primacy of events and proper names in favor of long periods and the lives of the anonymous. In this way history has claimed its place in the ages of both science and democracy. A history is also, in the second degree, the narrative of those series of events attributed to proper names. And the narrative is normally characterized by its uncertainty with regard to the truth of the related events and to the reality of the subjects to which they are attributed. Things would be too simple if one could say of any history, as the expression goes, that it is only a story.[1] The distinctive feature of a history is that it may always be either a story or not a story. Things would also be too simple if the certainty of the events went along with that of the subjects. But it is

1

always quite possible to attribute true events to fictitious or substitute subjects and uncertain or fictive events to real subjects. Fictionalized history and the historical novel both live the twists and turns that this indeterminacy authorizes.

Apparently, we no longer have these problems. Historical science has been constituted against fictionalized history and the historical novel. It was for this purpose that historians of the old school extolled the rigorous inspection of sources and the criticism of documents. It was for this purpose that historians of the new school have studied up on geography, statistics, and demography. Thus the materials of construction in historical study had to be sheltered from the fables of opinion and the twists of hack writers. What remains is that the materials are nothing without the architecture. We know that, in the usual sense of the expression—to know something is not to have to think about it. What we avoid considering is simply this: history is, in the final analysis, susceptible to only one type of architecture, always the same one—a series of events happens to such and such a subject. We may choose other subjects: royalty instead of kings, social classes, the Mediterranean, or the Atlantic rather than generals and captains. We are no less confronted by the leap into the void, against which no auxiliary discipline's rigors offer a guarantee: we must name subjects, we must attribute to them states, affections, events. And that is where the adherents of the chronicling tradition were already waiting, a century ago, for the partisans of a revolution in history, to warn them of the following: the objects and methods they advocated to get history caught up with science and the masses only made the rules of reference more indeterminable and those of inference more unverifiable. With the good old methods, regularly rejuvenated, it was possible to arrive at a sufficient degree of certainty about the acts of princes, their generals, and their ambassadors, about the thought that animated them, about the consequences of their policies, the reasons for the success or failure of the latter. With documents and their criticism, one may separate the series of events seriously attributable to Louis XIV or Napoleon from the challenges that deny the existence of the one or the fabrications about the other's twin brother. But how will the rigor of statistical series ever even allow the historian to support, without risk, a claim that the bourgeoisie has experienced some state, that the proletariat has known some evolution, or that the Mediterranean has undergone some event? To distance ourselves from the traditional subjects of history and from the means of verification attached to their visibility is to penetrate a terrain where the very meaning of a subject or an event is shaken, along with the manner in which we may make reference to the first and draw an inference from the second. How do we understand, for example, this typical sentence from the new history: "More than once did the conquering desert enter into the Mediterranean"?[2] Surely the historian of the scientific age would like to turn away from the convenient and superficial visibility of great events and great personages. But the more certain science that he claims is also a more improbable history, a history that pushes to the limit the indeterminacy of the referent and of the inference that belong to all history.

A question of words, one might say. An unfortunate homonymy in the French language designates lived experience, its faithful narrative, its lying fiction, and its knowledgeable explanation all by the same name. Exact in their pursuit of the traps of this homonymy, the English distinguish *story* and *history*. Concerned with exploring in their specificity the depth of lived experience and the conditions of the construction of discourse, the Germans separate *Historie* and *Geschichte*. These conventional references may seal a number of gaps in methodological presentations; their virtue stops there. The homonym hunters do the same as the others: they attribute series of events to subjects. There is nothing else to be done, short of ceasing to write history. And the homonym hunters generally even belong to the school of the victims of homonymy, recognizing in the *Annales* the paternity of the scientific revolution in historical discourse. The reason for this is just as simple in its basis as it is paradoxical in its appearance. The confusion of language was in fact needed to measure the dilemma in its rigor: the new historical science could no longer be a history, and still had to be one. The difference between history as science and history as narrative was necessarily produced in the heart of narrative, with the latter's words and use of words.

For the battle of the new history was from the beginning waged on two fronts. Facing the old school, which prided itself on bringing to history the greatest possible certainty, stood the good and the bad apostles of science, leaning over the cradle of the new history. And of course they encouraged the new history to take the step that would decisively place it on the terrain of scientific certainty—to abandon events, their insignificant succession, or their random causality; and to substitute facts—facts that are no longer attributable to any particular subject but that may be observed in their repetition, classified according to their properties, and correlated with other facts of the same type or other types of facts. And they indicated all the means for finding the sources and utilizing the methods appropriate to these new objects. The new history would be honored for having followed the lessons of the statisticians through the intervention of the sociologists and economists. It would acknowledge its debt to the incitement of a Simiand, assailing the three idols of the old history: the political, chronological, and individual idols. But well before Simiand, an obscure philosopher named Louis Bourdeau polemically sketched, in a hefty volume published in 1888, the emblematic setting of the new history: the great sea, barely rippled by the wind, opposing the calm of its depths to the wavelets of individuals and events. What, he asked, was the real amplitude of the most shattering events? The French Revolution didn't exist for four hundred million Chinese, and even in France, "the voices of the most ardent tribunes and the cannons of the most resounding victories"[3] did not make it to the deepest layers of the population. "In some distant valley, in many a peaceful village, there was not even a word about those events whose sound seemed to fill the world."[4] But we need not even speak of distant valleys. At the supposed center of the upheaval, the event slid across the surface of things:

> Whatever the events, everyone continues his customary trade: seeding, harvesting, manufacturing, selling, buying, consuming according to need and habit. . . . During the darkest days of the Reign of Terror, twenty-three theaters prospered in Paris. One company performed the opera *Corisandre* "with its charms," and others sentimental or comic plays; the cafés were full of people, the promenades very crowded.[5]

The conclusion was self-evident:

> For whoever contemplates the general order and entire sequence of the facts, there is no particular accident that does not seem worthy of study. These are, on the ocean of human affairs, fluctuations of waves that efface one another. The fisherman whose boat they lift

believes that he sees around him mountains and chasms; but the observer who casts his eyes into the distance, from the shore, sees only a smooth surface, barely wrinkled by the flow, terminated at the horizon by an immutable line.[6]

To take this immobile yet shifting horizon line of history into consideration was to study those "phenomena of function"—which would later be called facts of "material civilization" and phenomena of "mentalities"—attached to the great constants of human activity: those that concern the necessity of eating, producing, exchanging, or transmitting, but also of laughing and loving, of knowing and creating. The task of history was to follow the barely perceptible movement that tore those activities from the order of routine to throw them into the universe of invention. For this history, like every science, had to have its Copernican revolution. It had to turn toward "the most important personage of history, the hero who must be honored before all others . . . , the throng of the unknown."[7] This unperceived labor of genuine heroes and unknown inventors had to be recognized where it spoke its own language: the language suited to the activity of the anonymous multitudes, that of numbers and functions.

The science of human facts, for so long descriptive and literary, is destined to become entirely quantitative. The phenomena of function, the essential objects of study of this science, are in effect measurable by the two modes, the arithmetic and the geometric, of the determination of size. We may, on the one hand, translate size into number, and on the other, we may depict it for the eyes through graphic representation (in diagrams or cartograms) in which we summarize, in striking images that take the place of a universal language, long series of facts whose variations, relations, and laws appear in the full light of day. The ideal of history elevated to the dignity of science would be to express all its notions in this way, and no longer to employ words to explain and comment on these formulas.[8]

This would be the ideal of a historical science released from the indeterminacy of the words and phrases of stories, thus capable of transforming into real cognition what was still only the "novel of human life." This science wouldn't be in the least confined to the mere data of population, production, and commerce. It would on the contrary bear witness to the opening of an intellectual history established on a more meaningful basis—the statistics on diplomas, the book trade, or libraries; or a history of feelings and morals examined where they speak plainly—in the statistics on marriages or the analysis of wills.

Wasn't this the same revolution that Lucien Febvre wanted to proclaim by tying the scientific primacy of demography to the new political royalty of the *demos?* Wasn't this the same discourse that Fernand Braudel would later conduct on the deceptive obscurities and glimmers of the event, or Pierre Chaunu on the capacity of serial history to integrate all of human reality into the network of its correlations? Was the obscure Bourdeau an unrecognized precursor to whom the triumphant history of the *Annales* would show no thanks? We must answer negatively. The *Annales* historians were not ungrateful, but clear-sighted. They understood what the physicians of the scientific age proposed to them, in the guise of a remedy of rejuvenation: the means to a euthanasia. Inviting historical science to substitute the universal language of mathematics for the deceptive language of stories was inviting it to die painlessly, without acknowledging that this was being done. What the statistics on long periods would furnish to the future would be the elements of a comparative sociology. History would be no more than the diachronic dimension, useful in certain cases for explaining residual social phenomena. History, promoted to scientific dignity, was in fact a history that had vanished in the great science of the social, which provided the former an object and prescribed it a means of cognition. It was not only the sarcastic enemies of scientific history, but also its benevolent advisors, the economists and sociologists of the Durkheimian school, who deep down thought this way.

The distinctive feature of the revolution in historical study, then, does not simply consist in knowing how to define the new objects—long periods, material civilization, and the life of the masses—and how to adapt the new instruments of the language of numbers. It consists in knowing how to recognize, in the siren song of the scientific age, the threat of ruin of historical study, the dilemma hidden under the propositions of its scientificization: *either* history *or* science. It consists in knowing, in response to this dilemma, how to maintain the play of homonymy, because it alone was capable of transforming the disjunction into a conjunction: science *and* history. And this means: nonhistory and history, the power of articulation of names and events that is tied to the ontological indeterminacy of the narrative, but that nevertheless is alone suited to preserving the specificity of a *historical* science in general. The revolution in historical study is the arrangement of a space for the conjunction of contradictories. We do poor homage to this invention by admiring the diplomatic titles of the theses of Lucien Febvre and Fernand Braudel: *Philippe II et la Franche-Comté, The Mediterranean and the Mediterranean World in the Age of Philip II.* They thought, and allowed it to be thought, that they thus accorded their new scientific interest—the history of the great spaces of life formed over long periods—the reverence due their old masters, who applied themselves to great names and diplomatic history. But this art of conjunction does not depend on the simple rules of caution or of academic reverence. The *and* that ties the interests and investigations of the new history to the proper names of kings is not a matter of rhetoric. It is the specific response to an *either . . . or. . . .* It is not a simple matter of words. It belongs to a poetic elaboration of the object and the language of knowledge. The particular genius of Lucien Febvre is that he understood the following intuitively: history could conduct its own revolution only by making use of the ambivalence of its name—challenging, in the practice of language, the opposition of science and literature. It wasn't simply that one could reconcile the rigors of the one with the charms of the other. It was rather, much more profoundly, that only the language of stories was suited to the scientificity proper to historical science: a matter not of rhetoric, putting the young science in accord with the prejudices of the old masters and the rules of the institution, but of poetics, constituting, in the language of truth, the language—as true as it is false—of stories. The secular battle of historians with the old word history does not concern the accounts that every young science must settle, for a long time to come, with its ideological prehistory. It is the very principle of this word's proper dynamic: the interminable and interminably polemical adjustment of the vocabulary of naming, of the grammar of attributions, and of the syntax of conjunctions and subordinations that permit the language of stories to make use of its indeterminacy so as to suppress the latter, to negate itself in order to promote the impossible adequation of science and narrative, the equivalence of the time of the event and the time of this suppression.

The following pages are an attempt to study a number of singular knots in this constitution. Why has this constitution been insistently effected around several exemplary objects and figures? How have these become part of the plot? What is the relation between the logic of such plots and that of a certain number of syntactic usages—of the ways of disposing of subjects, of complements and attributes, of using conjunction and subordination, of the present and past of verbs, of their presence and absence? The question at stake is not that of the style of the historians, but of the signature of science. The signature is not the personalized appendix of a discourse, but the mark of its identity, the proper name that puts together proper nouns and common nouns, words and things, the order of the speakers and that of the objects of cognition. Such a study falls under what I have chosen to call a *poetics of knowledge*, a study of the set of literary procedures by which a discourse escapes literature, gives itself the status of a science, and signifies this status. The poetics of knowledge has an interest in the rules according to which knowledge is written and read, is constituted as a specific genre of discourse. It attempts to define the mode of truth to which such knowledge is devoted—not to provide norms for it, nor to validate or invalidate its scientific pretense. It doubtless concerns those so-called human or social sciences that, for centuries, have tried with varying amounts of luck to win their place in the accord of true sciences, to remove the interminable suspicion that they still belong to the works of literature or politics, even to both at the same time. But the poetics of knowledge does not set out to confirm this suspicion, to take history or sociology away from their scientific ambitions, back to their literary procedures and political presuppositions. The human and social sciences are children of the scientific age: the age of a certain number of decisive revolutions in the fundamental sciences; but also the age of scientific belief, the age that conceives of the rationality of every activity according to a certain idea of scientific rationality that has no necessary connection to the revolutions in question. But—we forget this too easily—the age of science is also that of literature, that in which the latter names itself as such and separates the rigor of its own action from the simple enchantments of fiction, as with rules on the division of poetic genres and procedures suited to belles lettres. It is finally—we "know" this more and more—the age of democracy, the age in which democracy appears, even in the eyes of those who combat or fear it, as the social destiny of modern politics; it is the age of broad masses and great regularities that lend themselves to the calculations of science, but also that of a new disorder and arbitrariness that disturb objective rigors.

The new history belongs to this age and this configuration. And it holds a highly singular place here. Among the poor relatives of science, it would at first seem to play the role of the poorest cousin, doomed, in spite of its entire statistical apparatus, to all the approximations of natural language, the confusions of opinion, and the seductions of literature. If it nonetheless often has the role of torchbearer, that is not by sole virtue of the weight conferred on it by the advanced age of its institution. This is rather because the radicality of its impoverishment has led it to explore more radically the powers available to language, so as to allow science and literature to be seen, as it effects its own abolition. And because it has strictly maintained itself in the space of homonymy of science and nonscience, because it has kept the name of the stories told to children and of the community legend taught to students in school, history has been able to lead straight to the impossible task of articulating three contracts in a single discourse. The first is a scientific contract, which necessitates the discovery of the latent order beneath the manifest order, through the substitution of the exact correlations and numbers of a complex process for the scale of the visible weights and sizes of politics. The second is a narrative contract, which commands the inscription of the structures of this hidden space, or of the laws of this complex process, in the readable forms of a story with a beginning and an end, with characters and events. And the third is a political contract, which ties what is invisible in science and what is readable in narration to the contradictory constraints of the age of the masses—of the great regularities of common law and the great tumults of democracy, of revolutions and counterrevolutions, of the hidden secret of the multitudes and the narration of a common history readable and teachable to all.

How do we keep these three requirements together, the first two of which seem to contradict each other completely and the third of which exemplifies and enlivens the contradiction? To grasp this articulation at the heart of the revolution in historical study, we must enter the workshop of the historian.

The Dead King

Let us then consider a singular narrative, borrowed from the exemplary book of the new history, *The Mediterranean and the Mediterranean World in the Age of Philip II*. In the last chapter of the book, just before the conclusion, Braudel tells us of an event, the death of Philip II.

He relates it to us, or rather he tells us why he has not related it to us in the normal order of the narrative: "We have not mentioned in its proper place one piece of news which quickly travelled to every corner of the world: the death of Philip II of Spain, which occurred on September 13, 1598. . . . "[1]

He therefore relates something to us that he has not related in its place, according to the order of the event and the narration: a scene that should have ended the narrative and did not. And we may easily understand the reason. The thousand and some preceding pages have explained it to us sufficiently: the end never took place. The noise that spread across the sea and the world doesn't refer to any event in their history, the history of the swinging motion that displaces the heart of the world from the Mediterranean to the Atlantic.

If the death of the king of Spain and Portugal is not an event in the history that the historian treats, two solutions seem to offer themselves to him. The first would be not to speak of it at all; and the second to speak of it in order to explain that there is no place to recount what, on the new terrain of history, no longer has the value of a significant event.

Now, Braudel chooses a third solution—the least logical one, it seems, as much from the point of view of science as from that of narration: he is going to recount this event that is a nonevent, outside the location and place that should have belonged to it. The logic of this illogicality is no doubt clear: to displace the event, put it at the end, at the edge of the blank space that separates the book from its conclusion, is to transform it into its own metaphor. We understand that the displaced death of Philip II metaphorizes the death of a certain type of history, that of events and kings. The theoretical event on which this book closes is this: that the death of the king no longer constitutes an event. The death of the king signifies that kings are dead as centers and forces of history.

This event may be explained. The historian chooses to relate it, to relate the death of a king as the death of the royal figure of history. The principle of the narrative will therefore be to substitute one narrative for another, to attribute to the subject Philip II a series of events other than his own. Told by the new historian, the death of King Philip II will not be his becoming-corpse but his becoming-silent.

From one paragraph to the next, then, the movement of the narrative takes us from the ceremonial of the last days of the king to the portrait of the king in all his majesty. The dead king on whom the narrative will be completed is not a king on his deathbed, but rather a king seated on his throne or at his desk. This is where he is metaphorically put to death, convinced not to speak, to have nothing to say. He is dead, then, like the letter, silent like the painting whose empty solemnity Plato's *Phaedrus*, for an age that is not over, opposed to the virtue of living discourse.

Here then is the portrait of the king on display: "We historians approach him rudely: he receives us as he did his ambassadors, with the utmost courtesy, listening to us, replying in a low and often unintelligible voice, never speaking of himself at all."[2]

So he is a silent king, or a paper king. The historian now shows him to us at his worktable, annotating the reports with his hasty writing—we may say, as good Platonists, with his silent writing. What he thus annotates is doubtless material for the old history, diplomatic dispatches on the events of court and the humors of kings. In the portrait of the king outlined in this way, how do we not recognize equally—by changing the angle of view, as with those grooved portraits that metamorphose according to the position of the observer—the portrait of the old academic, the illustrious Seignobos, or some other whipping boy of the new history?

> He is not a man of vision: he sees his task as an unending succession of small details. Every one of his annotations is a small precise point, whether an order, a remark, or the correction of a spelling mistake or geographical error. Never do we find general notions or grand strategies under his pen. I do not believe that the word Mediterranean itself ever floated in his consciousness with the meaning we now give it, nor that it conjured up for him the images of light and blue water it has for us. . . . [3]

The death of the king is therefore the leave given to a personage in whom we will recognize, as we please, the king or his historiographer: a man of letters or of paper, a silent one whose silence is particularly manifest in his not knowing what the sea signifies.

We may read in this scene the mere metaphor of a Copernican revolution in history: a displacement from the history of kings to that of the sea, understanding in the latter the history of the spaces of civilization, of the long periods of the life of the masses and of the dynamics of economic development. But, before we can know what a metaphor signifies, we must first determine what it consists of, what is literal in it and what figurative. That is where the difficulty begins and where the singularity of the text keeps us: what is real in this narrative and what is symbolic? Which events happen, and to whom? We understand how this particular characteristic—that the king speaks in a low voice—can symbolize the fact that the discourse of kings does not have much to teach us about the history of the world. But did King Philip II speak in a low voice? Is this a trait we ascribe to him from the testimony of chroniclers and ambassadors? Or from the sealed lips of Titian's portrait? Or even from the bass that Verdi assigned his voice, borrowing from Schiller the portrait of a king associated with the sepulcher, buried alive in his Escorial? The historian's text will not allow us to know—any more than it will say exactly how we may recognize the rapid quality of the sovereign's writing, and still less the reasons that make the historian assume that the Mediterranean evoked for the king neither sun nor blue water. Each of the individual traits charged here with symbolic value could just as well be the trait of an allegory deliberately composed by the new historian to say good-bye to the old history. The text is undecidable on this point. The historian doesn't give us the means to define the status of his assertions. By marking the distance that every citation of sources introduces between himself and the historical personage, the historian annihilates the effect of the text, which is completely insistent on collapsing that distance. In effect, the scholar's voice, taking stock of a reign and of the history of kings, is also that of an interlocutor to the sovereign, attracted in his familiarity by an intoxicating amphibology: "We historians approach him rudely: he receives us as he did his ambassadors. . . . " Certainly we understand that the historian is playing on the literal and figurative meanings of the word *approach*. No reader would be led to think that the reception is real and that Fernand Braudel actually met Philip II. She would wonder on the other hand what this presence of the historian in the picture would mean, on the same plane as the ambassadors, purveyors of the documents of the old history. What is the meaning of the historian's insistence on being represented in the scene, interrogating the king, waiting near his desk, leaning over him as he writes, and even, in other passages, just sitting down on the king's couch or in front of his papers?

Can we say that this is a figure of style? Or a historian's atavism, which pushes the most iconoclastic among them, as soon as a king passes within reach of their pen, to compose portraits, scenes, and moralities in the manner of a Saint-Simon? But the question is knowing what *style* means here. And the reference to the memorialist precisely marks the difference. The chronicle of the confidant of kings was written in the past tense; the surprising presence of the historian in the king's study punctuates the sovereignty of the present in the narrative of the new history.

The scholarly revolution in history is manifested, then, by a revolution in narrative tenses. This matter has received, all in all, little commentary. Paul Ricoeur put himself to the task of showing how *The Mediterranean* was still in the realm of narrative plot. But he seemed to dissociate that demonstration from the question of the grammatical usage of tenses.[4] How can one not be struck, nevertheless, by the singularity of this usage with regard to Benveniste's analysis of the tenses of discourse and those of narrative? We know how Benveniste, in a text that has become a classic, opposed the systems of discourse and narrative according to two fundamental criteria: the usage of tenses and the usage of persons. Marked by the personal engagement of a speaker concerned with convincing the one to whom she speaks, discourse liberally uses all the personal verb forms — in contrast to narrative, whose preferred person, the third, in fact functions as an absence of person. Discourse also uses, with the exception of the aorist, all the verb tenses, but essentially the present, perfect, and future, that are related to its moment of utterance. Historical enunciation is conversely ordered around the aorist, imperfect, and pluperfect, at the exclusion of the present, perfect, and future. Temporal distance and the neutralization of the person give narrative its unfulfilled objectivity, to which is opposed the affirmative presence of discourse, its power of self-attestation.[5] Scholarly history, according to this opposition, may be defined as a combination in which the narration is framed by the discourse that comments on and explains it.

Now, the entire task of the new history is to deregulate the play of this opposition, to construct a narrative in the system of discourse. Even in the part of *The Mediterranean* pertaining to "events," the tenses of the discourse (the present and future) concur largely with those of the narrative. Elsewhere they impose their domination, giving the "objectivity" of the narrative the force of certainty that it needs to be "more than a story." The sudden event, like the fact of long duration, is stated in the present, and the relation of an anterior action to a posterior one is expressed as the latter's future.

This reorganization of the narrative cannot be reduced to the "artifice of style" that is, for Benveniste, the "present historic" of grammars. It is not a question of rhetorical turns of phrase but of the poetics of knowledge: of the invention, for the phrase in historical study, of a new regime of truth, produced by the combination of the objectivity of narrative and the certainty of discourse. It is no longer a matter of inserting recounted events into the fabric of a discursive explanation. The casting of the narrative in the present tense renders its powers of assertion analogous to those of discourse. The event and its explanation, the law and its illustration, are given in the same system of the present, as this passage from *Capitalism and Material Life 1400–1800* shows in exemplary fashion, illustrating with a pointed example the regular progress of epidemics over a long period: "There is another rule with no exceptions: epidemics *jump* from one human mass to another. Alonso Montecuccoli, whom the Grand Duke of Tuscany *sends* to England, . . . *will cross* from Boulogne and not from Calais, where the English plague . . . *has* just arrived."[6] The tense of the rule is identical to the tense of the event. And this identity goes along with another, that of the literal and the figurative: the ambassador who crosses the Channel and the epidemic that jumps have the same modality of existence. The new history aims to assure the primacy of things over words and to circumscribe the possibilities of each time period. But this discernment of the weight of things and the specificity of tenses can function only on the basis of a poetical principle of indiscernibility. The true discourse on the advance of the epidemics and the fictitious narrative of the meeting between the king and the historian stem from the same syntax and the same ontology. The literal and the figurative are seemingly indiscernible here, and the present in which the king receives the historian responds to the future past of the ambassador's voyage.

The singularities of the narrative of the king's death seem, then, explainable in terms of this linguistic reorganization. The death of the king represents a two-pronged operation. It marks the absorption of the system of narrative, a characteristic of the old history, into that of discourse, through which history may become a science; but also, conversely, the setting into narrative of the categories of discourse, without which operation the new science would no longer be history. The allegory-narrative, the narrative of the indiscernible, effects the exchange between the categories of discourse and those of narrative that allows the new history to be written on the death rite of royal chronicles. And the singular confrontation of the present historian with the dead king could sufficiently represent the revolution in the system of pronouns that responds to the revolution in the system of tenses. Around a *we* that the knowledgeable collectivity of historians borrows from royal majesty, there is an exchange of properties between the *he* that has been distanced from the narrative and the present *I* that sustains the discourse.

But the king, of course, is more than a pronominal function, more than the third person who belongs to the bygone times of the narrative. The king is also, especially, the one who is grounded to speak in the first person, the one who, in the majestic plural, identifies the singularity of his speech with the authority of legitimacy that exceeds it. He is especially a proper name and a signature that give order to an assemblage of speakers, of rules of legitimacy for speech and for the usage of nominations. The figuration of the king, of his speech and of his writing, is the point where the poetics of the knowledge-narrative becomes conjoined with a politics, where the legitimation of science meets the figures of political legitimacy.

Apparently, the conjunction does not present a problem: the false narrative of the death of Philip II conjointly signifies the impoverishment of princes as objects of history and of their ambassadors as sources of historical knowledge. In their place are enthroned what is absent from the king's mind and what the duke's ambassador avoids: the blue sea that makes the history of human beings and whose history the latter make in return; the masses on whom the epidemic jumps and the great regularities of collective phenomena. History elaborates the knowledge of these new objects, at the intersection of the data furnished by the sciences of space, circulation, population, and collective facts, at the junction of geography, economics, demography, and statistics. This scientific displacement responds to the displacement of a politics that no longer beats to the hour of kings, but to that of the masses.

Nonetheless, something in the picture resists this overly simple consequence of the delegitimation of kings in the face of the new legitimacy of scholarly history, something like a secret dissymmetry in the relation between the old and the new, in the quadrilateral of the king, the ambassadors, the historian, and the masses. This may be a singular status of the "good" object, the sunny blue sea, given in its absence to the mind of the king; or the masses who verify at their own expense the scientific law skirted by the ambassador; or even a persistence of the ambassador, received with the historian, and whose dispatches still indicate what makes them derisory. It may also be a singular complacency of the historian to represent himself in the picture, to linger in the king's study and to cast his gaze over the king's papers, in the manner of one of Edgar Allan Poe's detectives, as if some secret were at once revealed and hidden in the papers that the king annotates. We have assumed that these letters were ambassadors' dispatches on the spectacle and the secret of the courts. But in the preface to the book, where it is not a matter of allegorical narrative but of methodological exposition, the author cuts, with a strange incision, the denunciation of the traps of the history of events, and offers singular readings to the king:

> We must learn to distrust this history with its still burning passions, as it was felt, described, and lived by contemporaries whose lives were as short and as short-sighted as ours. It has the dimensions of their anger, dreams, or illusions. In the sixteenth century, after the true Renaissance, came the Renaissance of the poor, the humble, eager to write, to talk of themselves and of others. This precious mass of paper distorts, filling up the lost hours and assuming a false importance. The historian who takes a seat in Philip II's chair and reads his papers finds himself transported into a strange one-dimensional world, a world of strong passions certainly, blind like any other living world, our own included, and unconscious of the deeper realities of history, of the running waters on which our frail barks are tossed like cockleshells.[7]

Beginning with the discourse on the method of the history of events, as well as with the narrative of the end of the king, a single shift has caused two presents to coincide and has led the historian to the "place" of the king, in a location that is its own metaphor and where four personages meet again: the king, the historian, the poor—who take the place of the ambassadors—and the sea, here advanced entirely to the rank of metaphor. In this narrative-discourse of the method that matches the discourse-narrative of the event, the play of the literal and the figurative is ordered around another major amphibology, less incongruous but more enigmatic: the "Renaissance of the poor," that is, figuratively, the false Renaissance or the caricature Renaissance that is opposed to the true Renaissance, grasped in its essence; but also, literally, the Renaissance as it was lived by the "humble," as the latter apprehended, expressed, and misunderstood it from their inferior and backward position. But who exactly are these humble people, whom a future abruptly comes to introduce and who immediately disappear from the scene? Were they numerous enough in the sixteenth century to write their angers and their passions? Were they visible enough that their writings came to the attention of princes and accumulated on their desks? To the point where this mass of paper is sufficiently intrusive to constitute, above all else, the body of interpretation of which the historian must clear the royal archive and the writing of history? We will know nothing of this cumbersome mass of paper except its nonplace. What the historian here seems to propose to us, outside all determined reference, is a fable that unites the literal and the figurative of the amphibology: something like a Platonic *muthos* where the poor do not represent any defined social category but rather an essential relation with nontruth. The poor are those who speak blindly, on the level of the event, because the very fact of speaking is an event for them. They are those who are "eager" to write, to speak of others, and to talk about themselves. Eagerness is the common failing of those who do what they have no place to do. The poor speak falsely because they have no place to speak. The poor, in the allegory of the science of historical study, represent the obverse of the "good" object of knowledge, the masses. The masses pervert themselves by moving outside their place, by leaving the great regularities of their objectification in order to fragment and dissolve themselves into subjects who speak, who speak of themselves and of others. The poor are the objects of history who pretend to be its subjects or its historians, the masses in so far as they undo themselves, as they decompose into speakers. At the heart of the Copernican revolution that seemed to found the legitimacy of the science of historical study on the delegitimation of the royal word, on its emptiness, the "Renaissance of the poor" comes to introduce another emptiness, the simulacrum of "its" revolution that makes history revolve around the speech of anyone at all. This revolution of paperwork, at once invading the royal seat and the historian's workshop, defines a negative solidarity between the two.

How do we understand the enigmatic relationship that the allegory of the new history draws among the paperwork of the poor, the place of the dead king, and the perils that await the method of historical study? Perhaps an apparently lengthy detour is needed for that, as well as an interest in another royal death, this one conceptualized by a philosopher half a century after the peaceful death of Philip II, in two books that frame the violent death of Charles I of England: the first great regicide of modernity, the first to found its legitimacy politically. I am thinking here of Thomas Hobbes's *De Cive* and *Leviathan*, and especially of the chapters devoted to the causes of sedition. These chapters are able to hold our attention because, in the traditional framework of thought on sedition—imbalances and ailments in the body politic—Hobbes introduces a dramaturgy and model for conceiving the relation among the perils that sedition represents for politics and science.

Two essential traits define this new dramaturgy and oppose it to the tradition inherited from Plato and Aristotle. It is henceforth no longer a matter of the classification of regimes, and of the causes that transform one regime into another. It is a matter of the life or death of the body politic as such. The question no longer pertains to the laws of conservation of each singular regime and to the causes of its ruin, but to the laws that conserve the body politic, whatever it may be, and to those that also prompt its dissolution. Now—and this is the second distinctive trait—these much more radical effects are produced by causes that are apparently much weaker. Ancient thought reduces the multiplicity of the causes of sedition to two principal ones: the conflict of classes and the disequilibria in the distribution of powers. But the causes that produce the collapse of the modern body politic are much less than that. They are first of all opinions, affairs of poorly used words or of unwarranted phrases. The body politic is threatened by words and phrases that drag here and there, anywhere; for example, "You must listen to the voice of your conscience before that of authority," or again, "It is just to suppress tyrants." These pronouncements of self-serving pastors find only too many complacent ears. The ailment of politics is first the ailment of words. There are too many words, words that designate nothing other than the very targets against which they place weapons in the killers' hands.

Let us take, for example, a word such as *tyrant* or *despot*. Such a name is not in fact the name of any class or property. From two things, then, there arises one: the alleged despot whose death is called for is either a legitimate sovereign or a usurper. The political pact evidently commands obedience to the former. But it does not follow that there exists the *right* to revolt against the latter—since the latter is not a bad sovereign whose subjects could legitimately punish him. He is simply an enemy with whom no pact exists. The members of the body politic do not have a conflict of legitimacy with him but only one of war. *Despot* or *tyrant*, in both cases, is a word without referent, an illegitimate name, itself the fruit of a usurpation.

Politics, for Hobbes, is ailing from these names without referents, from these phrases that have no place to be but that nonetheless take shape for two reasons, thanks to two complicities. The first is that of the men of the word made flesh, those pastors who simply take the opportunity to call "despot" or "tyrant" the sovereigns who are opposed to the encroachments of their religion, those "epileptics" who find in the Book of the Faith the apologues or prophecies that work to enlist the simpleminded. The second is that of the writings that give life and consistency to the figure of the despot: the texts of the ancients and of their imitators filled with stories and despots, with theories of tyranny and with its misfortunes, with stories and poems to the glory of tyrant-killers. The second great ailment of the body politic is thus supported: the literary and antiquating *hydrophobia* that joins religious *epilepsy* to ruin, through words and phrases, the body of the sovereignty.[8]

Hobbes thus conceptualizes a "Renaissance" or "mass of paper" of the poor with a radical theoretical and dramatic status. What constitutes it are those parasitic voices and writings that not only invade the office of the sovereign but also overload his body (the true body of the people) with a ghost made of words without body (the ghost of someone to kill), and thereby give the dispersed multitude of *anyone at all* the attributes of the body politic.

The same illusion, then, assigns the body of the king an empty name (despot) and gives the multitude a name that fits only the sovereign body, the name people. In this way the extravagant scene of a fiction-politics is constituted, placing anyone at all in the position of the legitimate transmitter or receiver of a discourse of the people, patched together of biblical prophecies or ancient-sounding harangues, even of a mixture of the two, or of imitations and near-imitations of the two. The modern revolution, whose birth Hobbes is witnessing, could be defined as follows: the revolution of the children of the Book, of the poor who are "eager to write, to talk of themselves and others," the proliferation of speakers who are outside their place and outside the truth, gathering the properties of the two great bodies of writing lingering within their reach, prophetic epilepsy and mimetic hydrophobia. It is a revolution of paperwork in which royal legitimacy and the principle of political legitimacy find themselves defeated, fragmented in the multiplication of speech and speakers who come to enact another legitimacy—the fantastical legitimacy of a people that has arisen between the lines of ancient history and of biblical writing. Such is, in the time of Philip II and Hobbes, the paperwork of the tyrant-killers, the soldiers of God, and those impassioned by Antiquity; through its agency the homes of "legitimate" speech are multiplied, along with the catalogs that allow for the changing of names and for the construction of figurations and argumentations that cause to appear, in one place or another, under one or another set of characteristics, despotism or freedom. The effect of this mass of paper is not simply a disturbance put in people's minds to prepare the way for the regicidal ax. It is, more profoundly, a first death of the king, a paper death that gives him a fantastical body, so that the attributes of his real body may be grasped.

Is it really necessary to link this philosophico-political scene with the historian's scientific scene under the slender pretext that both of them pertain to the matter of a dead king? Surely Braudel did not concern himself with all that. It is not a question, nevertheless, of knowing what he was concerned with. It is a question of the conditions in which the writing of the knowledgeable historical narrative takes place in the democratic age, of the conditions of articulation of the threefold—scientific, narrative, and political—contract. From this point of view, the relation of the two scenes does not express an approximate analogy but rather a well-determined theoretical knot. In the political and theoretical space opened by the English Revolution and the political philosophy of Hobbes, the death of the king is a double event, an event that ties, in their common peril, politics and science. The theoretical and political evil, for Hobbes and the tradition he opens, may be identified in this way: the proliferation of borrowed names, of names that do not resemble any reality, and that kill because they are poorly used, used by people who should not handle them, who have torn them from their context to apply them in a situation that has nothing to do with their context. The peril comes from all these floating names, from the multiplicity of homonyms and figures that don't name any real property but find, in their very motion, the means to incorporate themselves anywhere at all. The disorder of politics is strictly identical to a disorder of knowledge. The evil that the modern revolution sets to work is similar to that which metaphysics sets to work: it is that of words to which no determined idea is attached. Hobbes thus founds an alliance between the point of view of science and that of the royal place, a theoretical tradition that I propose to call royal-empiricism. This tradition will nourish the criticism of the French Revolution and of the "metaphysical" rights of man for which Burke will become the champion. But this tradition will also, in displacing political polemics onto scientific criticism, nourish an entire tradition of social science—that which tirelessly summons words in order to make them admit to the consistency or inconsistency of what they say, in order to denounce, in particular, the impropriety, the illusory homonymy of the words by which kings and royalties are set to action, in which the revolutions and great movements of the democratic age are made and stated. Since the event of the death of Charles I, this tradition has caused a suspicion, one that is both political and theoretical, to weigh on the politics of the modern age and on the history that is its child. Even when criminal imputation seems to be effaced in democratic consensus, the radical suspicion of nontruth persists and even proves fit to reawaken the ghosts of the primal scene.

The symmetrical oddities of the discourse on the paperwork of the poor and of the narrative of the royal death that open and close *The Mediterranean* are inscribed within the constraint of this theoretical and political space. The latter abolishes the nice image of a Copernican revolution, which made what revolved around the king simply revolve around the masses. It prohibits the mere coincidence between the leave given to kings and ambassadors and the promotion of a scientific history attached to solid and rigorously serviceable data from the life of the masses. To pass from the history of events to that of structures, one must separate the masses from their nontruth. Passing from royal chronicles to scholarly history is to encounter, on the king's table, a double mass of paper. There are the ambassadors' dispatches, the futile paperwork of kings' servants. And there is the paperwork of the "poor," of those who speak outside the truth, invading the lost time of history. Hobbes and the kings' enlightened partisans saw in this the weapon of death. Braudel, along with the clearheaded founders of modern social science, locate in it the "blindness" of life. There is no contradiction at all between these two judgments. It is on the contrary one of the founding axioms of modern social science, strongly punctuated by Durkheim: it is the excess of life that makes life sick—sick with blindness, blind to its sickness. It is the excess of life that provokes death. And the excess of life among speakers united in a society is first of all the excess of speech. This excess of words and phrases renders the peo-

ple of the age of the masses blind to the great equilibria and great regula-
tions that maintain the social body at the same time as they make it an
object of science. The excess of words that kills kings also strips the people of the democratic age of the recognition of the laws that keep their
societies alive.

We know how much this double threat has determined the sociological
project of a politics of knowledge. We also see how it gives its constraints
to the poetics of knowledge in historical study. The new history cannot
simply receive its new object from the death of kings. Like all legitimate
social science, it must regulate this excessive life of speakers that has
killed royal legitimacy and threatens that of knowledge. But, more so for it
than for any other social science, this requirement is crucial. Complicitous
by its very name with the sickness of speakers, intimately tied by its object
and its new aim to the death of kings and to the peril of legitimate speech,
it has the imperious obligation to rewrite the primal scene, to give the
kings another death through writing as well as a legitimate scientific succession. The figures of writing in historical study that collect in the narrative of the death of Philip II—the indiscernibility of the literal and the
figurative, the temporal royalty of the present, the exchange of powers of
discourse and narrative—then assume a determined sense. Far from any
"artifice of style," they respond to the challenge launched by the royal-
empiricist analysis of the king's death as a theoretical and political catastrophe. They efface the original stigma that casts as nontruth the forms of
knowledge proper to the age of the masses. To the paper-laden death of the
king, the allegory that they construct—homogeneous with scholarly narrative—opposes another paradigm of the royal death, fit to define a site of
nontruth for the history of the age of the masses. The poetics of knowledge
in historical study is the answer to a question on the politics of knowledge
that may be asked in its candor or in its brutality: how does one offer the
kings a good death, a scientific death?

The Excess of Words

The scene of the dead or silent king allows another scene to appear, this one equally crucial for the status of the discourse of historical study: that of a living person who speaks too much, who speaks incorrectly, out of place and outside the truth. The seriousness of the speech of historical study is challenged by this blind and blinding speech. The latter will be a chronicle or a history, literary or scholarly, according to the manner in which it will treat this event/nonevent of a speech whose subject does not have the capacity to guarantee the reference of what she says.

For this scene, as for the preceding one, the historian's choice is clearly circumscribed: she can refrain from speaking of a scientifically insignificant mass of paper. She can speak of it in order to explain why it does not have to be taken into account. Finally, she can remake the narrative according to what this writing says.

The choices are equally clear. The response will nonetheless be more complex. And we will measure this complexity by comparing two ways of treating speech out of its place, one borrowed from the tradition of chronicling and literature, and the other from modern scholarly historiography. Let's compare, then, the forms of speaking, in historical study, in two works that time, intention, and writing set at an infinite distance from each other, but that both pertain to the deceptive event of excessive speech:

Tacitus's *Annals* and Alfred Cobban's book *The Social Interpretation of the French Revolution.*

In the sixteenth chapter of the first book of the *Annals*, Tacitus tells us of a subversive event: the revolt of the legions in Pannonia, roused, the day after the death of Augustus, by an obscure agitator named Percennius. If this passage holds our attention, it is of course because it has already been the object of a masterful commentary, that of Erich Auerbach: in the second chapter of *Mimesis*, Auerbach comments on the representation Tacitus provides of a popular speech and movement, and opposes it to the one that, in the Gospel of Mark, the narrative of Peter's denial illustrates.

The singularity of Tacitus's narrative, marked by Auerbach, is the following: Tacitus meticulously reconstructs the argumentation of the legionary Percennius, with its concrete details and its persuasive force. But even before giving Percennius this convincing speech, he has declared it null and void. He has rigorously exposed the nonplace of his speech and he has strictly circumscribed the place of this nonplace: a vacancy, a time of suspension in military exercises. Augustus has just died. Tiberius is not yet on the throne. An objective void exists, which on the inside of the camp punctuates the general's decision: as a sign of mourning or rejoicing (we don't know which), he has interrupted the customary exercises. As a result something will happen that has no real cause, no profound reason, something that is the pure product of a void. The legions, with nothing to do, since it is well known that idleness leads to every sort of vice, "waxed wanton and quarrelsome, lent their ears to the discourses of every profligate, and at last they longed for a life of dissipation and idleness, and spurned all military discipline and labor." This forced leisure will be occupied by a specialist in leisure activities, a man of the theater, "one Percennius, formerly a busy leader of theatrical factions, after that a common soldier, of a petulant tongue, and from his experience in theatrical party zeal, well qualified to stir up the bad passions of a crowd."[1]

Before exposing the reasons for the revolt, Tacitus has thus indicated that there was no need to seek them. The vacancy from exercises alone erected the nonplace in the place, gave speech to the one who had no place to speak. Alone, it allowed, in place of the silence of military discipline, the erection of its exact opposite, the roar of urban theatrocracy.

Percennius had no place to speak. Nevertheless, Tacitus makes him speak. And his speech is ordered, precise, convincing. He paints the picture of the hardships of military life, the misery of those ten asses a day, the price at which they assessed their bodies and their souls, and out of which they still had to procure weapons, clothing, and tents, without counting the gifts they had to give the centurions to avoid duties and cruelties. He evokes the dupery of retirement, those lands generously allocated to veterans in the mire of swamps or on barren mountainsides. And his statement of grievances concludes with precise demands concerning salary and working time: "that their pay should be a denarius a day, sixteen years be the utmost term of serving; beyond that period [they should] be no longer obliged to follow the colors, but have their reward in money, paid them in the camp where they earned it."[2]

Thus the narration seems to be ordered according to a radical disjunction. The revolt is explained twice: in its absence of reason and in the reasons that it gives itself. And only the first has explanatory value. Not that Percennius's reasons are declared false; the historian doesn't comment on them, doesn't refute them. They are not said to be either true or false. They have, more fundamentally, no relation to the truth. Their illegitimacy is not due to their content but to the simple fact that Percennius is not in the position of legitimate speaker. A man of his rank has no business thinking and expressing his thought. And his speech is ordinarily reproduced only in the "base" genres of satire and comedy. It is ruled out that an essential conflict would be expressed through his mouth, ruled out that we would see in him, in a modern sense, the symptomatic representative of a historical movement that operates in the depths of a society. The speech of the man of the common people is by definition without depth. There is no more cause to explain Percennius's reasons than there is to refute them. There is only cause to restate them, in their proper coherence, in their affinity with the subject who pronounces them.

But to restate Percennius's reasons is by no means to repeat them. Moreover, who knows what Percennius could really have said? Surely Tacitus has no information on this topic. And it is without importance. Restating this discourse is not a matter of documentation but of invention, of knowing what a personage of this sort could have said in such a situation. And to do that we have, since Homer invented the much-imitated personage of Thersites, the appropriate models. After all, the statement of grievances and demands is too perfect in its argumentation, too well wrought in its expressions; one could never credit Percennius with the capacity to compose a similar one. Percennius doesn't speak; rather, Tacitus lends him his tongue, as he does elsewhere with Galgacus or Agricola. The statement is made up of pieces of rhetoric, composed according to the rules of suitability and plausibility, in imitation of models and to serve as models, in the schools, for other imitators. The only singularity here concerns the rank of the imitated personage. But the rhetorical tradition of imitation insists that, for purposes of narrative color and moral exemplification, one causes persons of varying dignity to speak, elevated to literary dignity before being returned to their proper place.

For Auerbach, this disjunction of the narrative is equivalent to a double dispossession: Tacitus strips Percennius of his reasons and his voice, of his belonging to a common history and his own speech. Auerbach opposes, to this rhetorical invalidation, the realism of the scene of Peter's denial in the Gospel of Mark: the presence of the "little" people, the character of the servant, the mention of Peter's Galilean accent—all of these dramatize the mixture of grandeur and weakness that characterizes the man of the common people seized by the mystery of the incarnation of the word. The mixing of genres—forbidden to Tacitus—allows the Evangelist to represent something that ancient literature could not depict, something that falls outside literature, and outside the divisions of styles and conditions that it presupposes. Thus Auerbach marks, in his own way, the relation between a politics of knowledge and a poetics of narrative, around the question of the representation of the other. Because he cannot take seriously the speech of a man of this rank and because he thinks in the categories of the division of noble and base genres, Tacitus falls short of the conditions of possibility of a literary realism that the evangelical narrative, on the contrary, opens. Auerbach's demonstration bears particularly on the aspect of the categories of poetics that concerns the separation of genres as a function of the dignity of the persons represented. He leaves the other aspect in the background, the one that pertains to what Plato names *lexis*: the modality of the poem's enunciation, of the relation between its subject and what it represents, a modality that varies beginning with the objectification of the *diegesis* in which the narrator tells a story, until the lie of *mimesis* where the poet hides behind his characters. Now, the importance of these categories of ancient poetics is that, in cutting across the modern linguistic categories of discourse and narrative, they authorize another type of questioning concerning this narrative and historical narrative in general. What relations of discourse and narrative make possible history in general and one or another of its forms? How is the inscription of excessive, illegitimate speech in accord with the system of these relations? With the system of persons that puts the narrator in relation with those who make him speak? With the modes and tenses of the writing of this speech, the effects of affirmation and objectification, of distance and suspicion, that belong to discourse or to narrative, to one form or another of their conjunction or disjunction?

According to this perspective, what will interest us in Tacitus's discourse is not its effect of exclusion, underscored by Auerbach, but, on the contrary, its power of inclusion: the place it gives, through its own agency, to what it declares to have no place. Percennius is not, for Tacitus, among those whose speech counts, to whom his fellows speak. And nevertheless he makes Percennius speak in the same mode as the others. He gives him speech in this "indirect style," which is the specific modality according to which he effects the equilibrium of narrative and discourse, and holds together the powers of neutrality and those of suspicion. Percennius speaks without speaking, in the infinitive mode, which is the zero-degree of the verb, expressing the value of information without deciding on the value of this information, without situating it on the scale of the present and the past, of the objective and the subjective. The indirect style, in practice disjoining meaning and truth, in effect cancels the opposition between legitimate and illegitimate speakers. The latter are just as much validated as suspected. The homogeneity of the narrative-discourse thereby constituted comes to contradict the heterogeneity of the subjects it represents, the unequal quality of the speakers to guarantee, by their status, the reference of their speech. Although Percennius may well be the radical other, the one excluded from legitimate speech, his discourse is included, in a specific suspension of the relations between meaning and truth, in the same way as that of the Roman chieftain Agricola or the Caledonian chieftain Galgacus. This equality of the speakers reflects another that defines the very texture of the history written by Tacitus. It reflects the homogeneity between the *stating* of history and the *stating* of what it recounts. To write history is to render equivalent a certain number of situations of discourse. Relating the action of Pericles or Agricola is an act of discourse that has the same status as the harangues of Pericles or Agricola. By recasting their discourses as one might suppose that they effected them, the historian also produces the material of a whole series of discursive functions: providing a diversion for the educated, lessons in politics for princes and heads of state, lessons in rhetoric and morals for students in the schools. What Pericles says to the Athenians, what the rhetoric teacher teaches the student in school, what the historian writes by repeating the words of Pericles according to the models of his teacher—all of this has the same status, is situated in the heart of a universe of homogeneous discourse. This homogeneity does not prevent an occasional denunciation of the lie of words—Thucydides does it, and Tacitus has it done through Galgacus. But the suspicion cast on the speech of the other regulates itself through the rhetorical form of the disjunction of meaning and truth, the suspension of reference. It does not create a double basis, a metalanguage that confronts discourse with its truth. The discourse of Thucydides denouncing the orators of the cities is of the same nature as those by which the latter mutually denounce one another. The preliminary disqualification of Percennius liberates the power, equal to any other, of his statements. And the exaggeration that Galgacus himself commits, by calling a desert that which the Romans baptize with the deceptive name of peace, is included in the same play of language that includes him, a foreigner, just as it includes, in the person of Percennius, the one who can't partake in any language. The language to which the latter has no right, in giving itself the right to make him speak, includes him in its community. The disqualification that strikes him is redeemed by the very confidence in language, in the indistinct powers of the speaker. Galgacus doesn't speak Latin, Percennius said nothing that fame has preserved. What nonetheless remains is the gathering power of language and of the play that it authorizes, the power of a discourse that is always susceptible of allowing entry into its community of those excluded when its circle is drawn.

The appropriation of the other's speech, then, can be reversed. By invalidating the voice of Percennius, substituting his own speech for the soldier's, Tacitus does more than give him a historical identity. He also creates a model of subversive eloquence for the orators and simple soldiers of the future. The latter will henceforth not repeat Percennius, whose voice

has been lost, but Tacitus, who states the reasons of all those like Percennius better than they do. And when the language of Tacitus has, as a
dead language, taken on a new life, when it has become the language of the
other, the language whose appropriation procures a new identity, the overly talented students in the schools and seminaries will fashion, in their own
language and in the direct style, new harangues; the self-taught will in
their turn take these as models, competing with the evangelical narrative
and the imprecation of the prophets. All who have no place to speak will
take hold of those words and phrases, those argumentations and maxims,
subversively constituting a new body of writing. Regicidal *hydrophobia*
and the *metaphysics* of human rights feed each other, to the despair of
Hobbes and Burke, to create the scene of the modern revolution, of the
revolution of the children of the Book.

This despair, we have said, did not remain sterile. It created of itself a
tradition of modern social science. It created this tradition in an essential
relation with the misfortune of the revolutionary event: a relation that
identifies this political misfortune with the misfortune—with the infelici-
ty—of the words used out of their context. If the revolution (and most particularly the French Revolution) played for social science (and especially
for sociology and history) the two-sided role of founding event, its violence is identified with the theoretical scandal of the event in general. This
scandal of the event is that of the conflagration of discourses and the confusion of time periods. Every event, among speakers, is tied to an excess of
speech in the specific form of a displacement of the *statement*: an appropriation "outside the truth" of the speech of the other (of the formulas of
sovereignty, of the ancient text, of the sacred word) that makes it signify
differently—that makes the voice of Antiquity resonate in the present, the
language of prophecy or of belles lettres in the common life. The event
draws its paradoxical novelty from that which is tied to something restat-
ed, to something stated out of context, inappropriately. The impropriety of
expression is also an undue superimposition of time periods. The event has
the novelty of the anachronistic. And the revolution, which is the event par
excellence, is par excellence the place where social science is constituted
in the denunciation of the impropriety of the words and of the anachronism
of the events. It is not at all through appropriate polemic but through theoretical necessity that the interpretation of the French Revolution put in its

heart the question of anachronism and pursued it to its limit—that affirmation of the nonplace of the event that bears the name revisionism.

The original ghost of social science is the revolution as anachronism, the revolution in the clothing and discourse of antiquity. The revolution makes a common event and disruption out of the anachronism, out of the temporal distance from the speaker that is her defining characteristic. The challenge that it thereby mounts to politics and thought have been placed by social science under a specific form: in the elaboration of a way of thinking about time that is not concerned with events, about a time liberated from the anachronism of speech and of the event.

Among these reelaborations of time that occupied the age of revolutions, two played a determining role in the conception of social science and its critical vocation. The Marxist manner took as an essential axis the relation of the future to the past. The slowing of the forces of the future, their lack of maturation, was therein made responsible on each occasion for the regression, for the anachronistic and verbose repetition of the past in place of the execution of the tasks of the present. The ignorance of the historical actor and the symmetrical knowledge of the theoretician of history were linked to this predominance of a future, alone fit to explain the past, but always missing in the present of the action, always newly split in the inaccessibility of a *not yet* determining the repetition of a *once more*. The analysis of class struggle that was Marx's paradoxical glory is rather the theatrical distribution of the shapes that may be taken by the conjunction of the *not yet* and the *one more time*.[3]

Royal-empiricist analysis, today reinvigorated by the vicissitudes of the Marxist model, proceeds in the other direction, on the temporal axis, by the conjoint disqualification of the categories of past and future. The utopia that guides its interpretations is that of a science whose categories would be adequate to their object because they would be exactly contemporaneous with it. The present is its time. But the defining characteristic of the present—like that of the real—is that it conceals itself ceaselessly from those who have come to terms with it. It must thus always be regained over the past and the future, established by the incessant critique of the past that repeats itself out of season and of the unduly anticipated future. The interminable accounts that royal-empiricism has with the revolutionary event thereby pass through an interminable reinterpretation of the Marxist-futurist interpretation of the event's anachronism.

This reinterpretation is exemplified in Alfred Cobban's *The Social Interpretation of the French Revolution*, which has become a guiding light among books in the revisionist historiography of the French Revolution. Its title is obviously emblematic of this status. The labor of the historian is no longer to recount revolutions but to interpret them, to relate the events and discourses to what founds and explains them. And, of course, what founds the events always belongs to a nonevent; what explains the words is what no longer belongs to words. The historian, in short, assumes the task that Auerbach reproaches Tacitus with not being able to perform. She will see what is behind the words. She relates the seductive discourse to the nondiscursive reality that is therein expressed and disguised. The historian's discourse is a measuring discourse that relates the words of history to their truth. That is explicitly what *interpretation* means. But it is also, less evidently, what *social* means. *Social*, then, designates at once an object of knowledge and a modality of this knowledge. In one sense, the "social" interpretation of the French Revolution is the analysis of revolutionary processes in terms of social relations and conflicts. It measures these processes on the scale of their significance and effect in this realm: the transformation of the status of property, the distribution and conflicts of the social classes, their ascent, their decline, or their various mutations. But this first sense is immediately surpassed by another: the social becomes this *base* or background of the events and words that must always be extracted from the lie of their appearance. *Social* designates the distance of words and events from their truth, which is nonverbal and does not pertain to events. From the outset social interpretation poses a certain geography of places: there are facts that do not belong to the discursive order but require a discursive act, none other than interpretation. But between the facts and the interpretation there is an obstacle to overcome, a thick cloud of words to dissipate. The transformations in French society produced by the Revolution are obscured by the mass of words of and on the Revolution: the words of the revolutionary actors, of the hagiographic historians, of the republican tradition, of the Marxist interpretation in terms of the bourgeois revolution, of the combination of those diverse traditions in the historiography of the likes of Mathiez and Soboul. Interpretation has to do with the excess of words *of* the Revolution and *on* the Revolution. *Social* interpretation is a matter of a first social interpretation: an interpretation that has already tried to substitute things for words but has let itself, in this very operation, be trapped by words.

It has let itself be trapped by words: this means that it employs words that are improper because they are not contemporary with what they name. For Cobban, Marxist interpretation sticks words and notions from later times onto the past event. But it can do this because it takes for granted the words of the actors, contemporaries, and chroniclers of the Revolution. Now, these words were themselves anachronistic. They referred to a situation that in fact no longer existed in their epoch. In short, Marxist interpretation believed the Revolution to be bourgeois because the revolutionary actors had believed that feudalism still existed, and that they were destroying it. If these misinterpretations—forward- and backward-looking—can exist simultaneously, it is because they rest on the same excess that belongs to human language in general, to human language before science put it in order: the fact that the same word could at once designate several entities and several properties, that it could designate properties that did not exist, but also properties that no longer existed or were still to come. The evil that social interpretation must relentlessly confront is that of homonymy.

The critique of homonymy, like the concept of the social, operates in a double register. It simply requires, on one level, that we give to the words that designate social identities the meaning they had in their epoch. In order not to misconstrue the class relations in the revolutionary era, we must, for example, know the following: a *manufacturier*, in this time, is not a major industrialist but simply someone who makes products with his hands; a *laboureur* is not an agricultural laborer, but a property-owning peasant, generally well off. A *fermier* is essentially someone who pays rent to work a plot of land but also to exercise a function. From these examples we see an entire task of rectification that may seem minor. All things considered, a good historical dictionary would suffice to restore these words to their exact meaning. We would then give all these relations their adequate names, conserving only their genuine, distinctive traits. But this terminological rectification finds its results, in their turn, threatened by the existence of a certain number of all-encompassing words that occupy the terrain without designating any distinct social reality. The most decep-tive words are evidently the ones most frequently used—nobles, bour-geois, peasants, for example. These words unite, in a monstrous conjunc-tion, properties that are not contemporaneous with one another, social relations that no longer exist and others that do not yet exist. Let's take the most deceptive word—*noble*. If in 1789 we look at a cross section of social positions, we will find nobles at all echelons of society and in the most diverse positions. This reality is unfortunately covered by images of court and castle, and in addition by the assimilation of the noblesse into feudalism, of seignorial rights into feudal rights. Here again, if we enter into the detail of the relations, the object designated by the name decom-poses. What we call "seignorial rights" is a heterogeneous assembly of rights of various origins, which does not define any personal dependence of commoners in relation to lords, does not define any properly feudal relation. Quite often they are mere property rights, and moreover frequent-ly bought up by bourgeois. It is impossible to name these rights feudal without "stretch[ing] the meaning of the term to a point at which it loses all historical meaning."[4] And this also goes, unfortunately, for each of the three orders convened at Versailles in the spring of 1789. None of them names a set of properties that gives a social meaning to its name. The classification of the noblesse, the clergy, and the third estate, well before 1789, ceased to have "any close relation" with their corresponding social realities.[5]

The double range of the word *social* may be specified as follows: *social* designates a set of relations. But it also designates the lack of words for designating them adequately. *Social* designates the nonrelation as a princi-ple. It designates the gap between words and things or, more precisely, the gap between *nominations* and *classifications*. The classes that name them-selves, and that are named, are never what classes must be, in the scientific sense: sets of individuals to which it is possible to attribute rigorously a finite number of common properties. The anachronistic and homonymic confusion requires that the words of history be names. A name identifies, it doesn't class. The evil is slight as long as the kings—whose names, with the exception of a few impostors, guarantee their identity—make the his-tory. It risks becoming irremediable when classes take the place of kings, precisely since these classes are not classes.[6] This constitutive defect is not simply the sin of Marxist interpreters. It is the sin of the very actors in the event, the sin by which events are produced—by which, simply, there is history. There is history because the speakers are united and divided by names, because they name themselves and name the others with names that don't have "any close relation" with sets of properties. What makes sense for them and what they make an event out of is precisely what, for the royal-empiricist historian, is "without relation"—it is the intricacy of what he asks us to distinguish: the juridical and the nonjuridical, the personal and the real, the past and the present, feudal privilege and bourgeois property. And this makes sense for those who act not as representatives of definite social identities through sets of properties but as nobles or knaves, bourgeois or proletarians—that is to say as speakers. A class or order is precisely a conjunction of these disjointed and noncontemporaneous traits. In the words *order* and *class*, a relation between the positions of the speaker and the social ranks is at play, which no set of distinctive traits will ever guarantee. There is history precisely because no primeval legislator put words in harmony with things. Pushed to its limit, the will to liquidate improper names comes down to the will to liquidate the impropriety and the anachronism by which events in general happen to subjects. The declaration of the "nonrelation" between the words of history and its realities is, finally, the suicide of the science of historical study.

This suicidal drive takes, in Cobban's text, a determinate shape. We must, he tells us, abandon the terminology of the Revolution—that of the actors and that of the interpreters—in order to examine the social facts as would a sociologist who was contemporary with the Revolution. The thesis is, at bottom, that the only relation between past and present carries within it the stigma of the false: noncontemporaneity, the impossibility of arresting the list of properties to render a word adequate to what it designates. For the historian to be within the true, she must work on the data of a contemporary sociologist who would permit her to grasp the exact social realities at once designated and hidden by the words of history.[7] But who is this sociologist, a contemporary of the event, whose science we are unfortunately lacking? Not a social scientist, but the utopian figure of social science itself: the primeval legislator who puts names in accord with their referents, the *present in the present* that conjoins the two significations, the two faces of the social, and liberates us from the chronic anachronism of the speaker? What is unfortunate, in this case, is that there is no sociologist contemporary with the French Revolution. And there is nothing accidental about this misfortune. It is because there was a French Revolution that sociology was born, born at first as the denunciation of the lie of words and events, as the utopia of a social realm adequate to itself.

In this recourse to an anachronistically contemporary sociologist, royal-empiricist criticism reaches the limit to which scientific belief pushes historical knowledge: that of the impugnment of its object. Deprived of a recourse to a symbolic language or to some metalanguage, critical history must nourish its scientistic desire for a perpetual suspicion of words. The impossibility of replacing the bad names with the good obliges it to signal itself as such by showing that none of the words corresponds with the reality that it designates. It obligates critical history to deny the possibility that there is an event, unless by impropriety. Ultimately, scholarly history is written as the nonplace of history. This limit has a theoretical name that is also a political name: it is called *revisionism*. Revisionism in history is not the circumstantial consequence of political biases or of the intellectual taste for paradox. It is the final term of this politics of suspicion by which the social sciences must exhibit their belonging to science—with even more force, since this belonging is increasingly contested. And the particular fragility of this history exposes it to the limit of this suspicion: the declaration of its object's nonexistence. The core of the revisionist formulation in general is contained in a simple formula: *nothing happened such as it was told*. The consequence of this is modulated differently, depending on whether one separates or brings together the nonrelation with the nothing that attracts it. The nihilist version of the formula deduces from it that *nothing happened of what was told*, which comes down to saying that nothing happened at all. Although it is propitious to political provocation, the conclusion is suicidal for history, whose lot remains, in spite of everything, suspended at the minimum requirement that, sometimes, something happens. After all, the politics of suspicion is rightfully extended to this very radicality. For the *nothing* toward which this politics causes the deceptive words of the event to tend has the flaw, even more than these words, of being a word that doesn't designate any property. The positivist practice of revisionism, opposed to the nihilist practice, is therefore content to incline the *no-such* toward the *almost nothing* of its effect or toward the *nonplace* of its cause.

It is in the direction of the *almost nothing* that Cobban's demonstration naturally tends. This direction does not state that the Revolution didn't take place or that it had no place to be, but that its consistent social effect is reduced to just a few things: some changes in the distribution of landed property, some modifications in the internal composition of the bourgeoisie, and a much more stable society than before. On the whole, it is quite fair to make of the French Revolution a convincing example of the infinite distance of words from things.

The direction of the *nonplace* is pursued in François Furet's demonstration in *Interpreting the French Revolution*. And the latter proceeds by a remarkable inversion around the question of the event. What it originally reproaches Marxist historiography with is effectively causing the question to disappear in the statement of its assumed social causes. The revolutionary event, that which we must not dissolve in the supposed effect of its causes, is precisely the opening of a new political space, characterized by an excess of spoken words. "The main characteristic of the Revolution as an *event* is a specific mode of historical action; it is a dynamic that one may call political, ideological or cultural, for its enhanced power to activate men and to shape events arises from an overinvestment of meaning."[8] This determination of the meaning of the Revolution is therefore initially situated in complete opposition to the nominalism and sociologism of Cobban. But the "overinvestment of meaning" invoked is also the object of a spectacular deflation. The "dynamic" of the revolutionary event then allows itself to be entirely summarized in two concepts that seem to come directly from the pages of Tacitus, those of *vacancy* and *substitution*. What provokes the radical revolutionary novelty, just like the fine discourse of the actor Percennius, is, properly speaking, a void. The Revolution as an unseen event is provoked by the "vacancy of power,"[9] it "takes over an empty space" beginning with an initial disappearance: "From 1787, the kingdom of France is a society without a State."[10] This vacancy of power requires the force that takes over to "restructure a fragmented society by means of the imaginary."[11] This obligation to occupy an empty space consequently institutes a replacement by "the reign of democratic rhetoric and domination of societies in the name of the 'people.' "[12]

The narrative plot of the critical historiography of the Revolution here seems to reproduce exactly the plot of Tacitus's narrative: the vacancy of authority provokes the proliferation of excessive speech. But this apparent similarity of the narrative sequences of ancient literature and of modern historical science covers a profound difference in the nature of their elements. The nonplace is the cause in both cases, but not in the same way. In Tacitus it remains a pure void. But critical historical science fills the void with a theory of the nonplace, which qualifies the substitution in terms of a theory of the imaginary and gives a very particular status of reality to the vacancy. Science first names the substitution, and it identifies it with the very concept of the other of science: illusion, the imaginary, ideology. The "overinvestment of meaning" is not only a word of excess, it is the specific misapprehension of the cause. "The revolutionary consciousness, from 1789 on, is informed by the illusion of defeating a State that has already ceased to exist. . . . From the very beginning it is ever ready to place ideas above actual history. . . . " It is this retrospective illusion that structures the imaginary of revolutionary radicality and permits it to transform the intersection of several heterogeneous series of events into "the inevitable consequence of bad government."[13]

This is the first fundamental difference between the two narratives. Tacitus related the accident of a vacancy with the nonplace of a spoken word. The illegitimacy of Percennius's assumption of the spoken word exempts him from any judgment on the illusory or truthful character of his statements. Scientific history, on the other hand, proves itself by qualifying its other. Speech is born from a vacancy; speech that has no place to be is necessarily a speech of illusion. But this visible mark of science conceals another, this one more secret and more essential. The difference in the effect of the nonplace is related to a difference in its cause, in the ontological status of the nonplace itself. In Tacitus, the vacancy refers to an event that may be empirically designated: Augustus is dead, the exercises have effectively been stopped. In contrast, the vacancy invoked by François Furet has the structural, not accidental, property of being unpresentable: "From 1787, the kingdom of France is a society without a State. . . . The revolutionary consciousness . . . is informed by the illusion of defeating a State that has already ceased to exist." What gives the illusion its force is, of course, that what it doesn't see is something that doesn't allow itself to be seen. Piraeus may, in spite of everything, be distinguished from a man, and the moon from green cheese. But nonexistence is the most difficult thing in the world to see. And the nonexistence of States is what States, in so far as they exist, have the task of disguising. It is not simply that the "traditional façade" still masks, in the eyes of the profane, "disorder within the walls."[14] It is rather that the symbolic walls are there to hide their own cracks. The statement according to which, from 1787 on, "the kingdom of France is a society without a State" is an unverifiable/unfalsifiable statement, a statement that produces in its referent a specific effect of suspension: not the rhetorical suspension of Tacitus that disjoins excessive speech from its truth but the scientific suspension that renders the narrative of the event indiscernible from the metaphor of science. What produces the excess of the speech event is the impossibility of seeing the void that causes the speech and that science alone sees. What science alone knows is that the king is already dead before being put to death, dead from another death. It is ignorance of this death, the latter invisible to every gaze but the scientific one, that prompts the illusion of combatting an already-dead king; and this illusion finds its logical conclusion in regicide and terror.

The explanation of the revolutionary event, then, comes into agreement with the categories of the royal-empiricist model: the nonplace, which brings about the vertigo of speech and the illusion that makes the event, always has the same cause. The historical actors live in the illusion of creating the future by combatting something that, in fact, is already in the past. And the Revolution is the generic name of this illusion, of this false present of the event that is the conjunction of a misapprehension and a utopia: the misapprehension of the past character of what one believes to be present, the utopia of making the future present. The Revolution is the illusion of making the Revolution, born from ignorance of the Revolution already being made.

The demonstration of this circle traverses two established and apparently contradictory interpretations of the Revolution: the liberal interpretation that inscribes it in the evolution of modern societies and shows it to have been prefigured from the very earliest times of the monarchy; and the counterrevolution that describes it, on the contrary, as a forceful blow that imposed, on an organically constituted society, the artificial order of philo-

sophical individualism and philosophical egalitarianism. The first tradition is the one that Tocqueville illustrates, showing the long progress of
equality in modern times going hand in hand with the achievement of
unification and monarchical centralization. According to this interpretation, it was the kings who forged the republican nation. The Revolution, in
1789, had already taken place. Thus Tocqueville can end his study before
1789, leaving to others the care of finding out why the revolutionaries set
themselves to making a revolution that no longer had to be made. It is precisely in this opening that the counterrevolutionary explanation can situate
itself. The latter has as its specific object the task of explaining how something took place that had no place to take place. And the principle of the
explanation is simple. It assigns as cause the existence of a body of spe-
cialists in the nonplace: the intellectuals. "A sociology of intellectuals,"
says François Furet to qualify the interpretation of Augustin Cochin on the
determining role of the *sociétés de pensée*. But here again the "sociologist" is simply the one who denounces the gap between words and things.
And in fact Augustin Cochin does nothing else than restore to sociology
the primal scene that the counterrevolution had given it as its birthplace:
the drama of the organic social bond torn apart by philosophical artificial-
ism and individualism. "Intellectuals" is the scholarly name that comes in
place of the political name "*philosophes*." And it is, indissolubly, the name
of a narrative function: that of the subjects who will bring the nonplace
into being. The two interpretations, then, intertwine: the imaginary Revolution of the future lasts through the interval necessary for society to
become aware that the Revolution is already in the past. "By making society once again independent from ideology, Robespierre's death takes us
from Cochin to Tocqueville."[15] "Thermidor separates not only two phases,
but two concepts of the Revolution. It marks the end of Cochin's
Revolution, and brings to light Tocqueville's Revolution."[16]

The formulation is worth pausing over. We understand, of course, that
neither Cochin nor Tocqueville made a revolution, no more than Philip II
ever received Fernand Braudel. We are therefore not deceived in the play
of amphibology and in the figures of equivalence of narrative and discourse. But here this equivalence, maintained in the narrative of the dead
king, falls entirely on the side of the discourse that absorbs the narrative,
of the interpretation that takes the place of the event. The play of comple-

ments effects the substitution of subjects, the substitution, for the historical scene, of the historiographic scene, in which the Revolution is the affair of actors other than those who believed they had made it, in which it no longer exists except as the entanglement of interpretations. The initial will to grasp the event by freeing it from the interpretations has thus precisely returned. The emblematic event of Thermidor is the completion of the illusory reign of the event, the pure limit separating two interpretations, two discourses of political science: an interpretation of illusion and an interpretation of reality. In this disappearance of history in historiography, the scholarly pretension of history, taken to the limit where its object is eradicated, comes to extend its hand to the scholarly pretension of politics. History, having become historiography, becomes a division of political science, a teratology or demonology devoted to the study of the aberration that causes the event of speech to proliferate through the cracks in political legitimacy. The end of the scholarly belief of historical study is the abolition of history, where it becomes sociology or political science. The completion of the scholarly revision of the Revolution perhaps signals the closure of the age of history.

By this very movement, this completion allows a return to within the age that it closes: the conquering age of history as a narrative of intelligibility articulating the triple—narrative, scientific, and political—contract in the interval between the old political art and the new science of the management of affairs. The age of history was that in which historians invented a conceptual and narrative framework that was suited to neutralize the excess of speech but also to master the death drive inherent in the scholarly belief in history. The age of history, from Michelet to Braudel, was that in which the historians were able to rewrite the scene of the king's death in the equilibrium of narrative and science.

The Founding Narrative

The scholarly history of the democratic age has a problematic genealogy. Lucien Febvre hailed Michelet as the founding father of the *Annales* school. But the obligatory homage leaves the meaning of this paternity unclear. And this ancestor is in truth burdensome. Well-trained historians have trouble seeing what the rigors and cautions of the method owe to the romantic historian's passions, phantasms, and effects of language. Thus they willingly leave to the semiologist the care of studying the conjunction.[1] We will attempt to show, on the contrary, that Michelet's "phantasms" and effects of style really define the conditions of the scientific speaking of the *Annales*, that they are the operators of what has recently been termed an epistemological break, of what I prefer to call a revolution in the poetic structures of knowledge.

What Michelet in effect invented, for the history of the age of the masses, is the art of treating the excess of words, the "death by paperwork" of the king. In the face of the royal-empiricist model, he invented a republican-romantic paradigm of history by which the latter must still conduct itself—as long as it wishes to remain a history and not a comparative sociology or an annex of economic or political science. The constitution of this paradigm assumes a narrative of the revolutionary event, a regulation of the revolutionary excess of speech, capable of at once suppressing and maintaining it in its status as speech event.

This regulation, in the *History of the French Revolution*, may be read in an exemplary narrative, a founding narrative, that of the Festival of Unity. The latter is, for Michelet, the peaceful and fundamental event where the meaning of the Revolution becomes manifest: not the destruction of the Bastille or the decapitation of the royal family but the appearance of a new political entity that is at the same time the new object of love, the native land. "At length the shades of night disappear, the mist is dispelled, and France beholds distinctly what she had loved and followed, without ever having been able to attain it—the unity of the native land. . . . The native land appears to them on the altar, opening her arms and wishing to embrace them."[2]

This is the event of which *we must* speak if we want to found a new history, detached from the old tradition of chronicling but also freed from the royal-empiricist resentment toward deceptive and murderous words. Lucien Febvre, at least, understood it perfectly: a new history of things is possible only on the condition that we hold fast to the reality of names and particularly to those names that succeed the name of the king—France, the native land, the nation, those "personified abstractions" denounced by the empiricist routine of the chroniclers.[3] To make possible a history of the age of the masses, one that does not bear on events, we must first speak of that event of a crowd assembled to celebrate the appearance of an incarnated abstraction. And we must speak of it in a way that does not dissolve that presence of a word to the crowd by decomposing the latter into its already given reality (the unity forged by royalty) and its ideological translation (the consensus forged by the drunken chattering of the *sociétés de pensée*).

How then do we recount this event so that it doesn't simply figure the void of ideology that is substituted for the void of royal power? So that it provides an originary place common to democratic politics and scholarly history? That is the problem to which Michelet brings a solution. What he invents to this end is the very principle of what we saw at work in Braudel's chapter on the death of Philip II, the principle of the new narrative, of the narrative that is not one and that thereby suits the event that doesn't have the character of an event. Michelet follows, to this end, a highly singular procedure. At first sight, he seems to refer us, for the narrative of the event, to the existing testimonies that by themselves seem to make it speak sufficiently. "Most of the federations," he tells us, "have themselves related their own history";[4] and he pursues the exceptional character of this literature, of these documents of an event that are thus at the same time the monuments of a new age: "Venerable monuments of youthful fraternity, . . . you will remain for ever as witnesses of the hearts of our fathers, and of their transports, when they beheld for the first time the thrice blessed face of their native land!"[5]

A new sort of document thus comes to make this event present: the entrance of the people from anonymity into the universe of speakers. In one sense, the document is identical to the event itself. The writings are by themselves the event of the appearance of the native land, the constitution of a new memoriality and historicity. And at first it seems that it is enough to let them speak: opening quotation marks, three *coups de théâtre*, announcing the voice of the new historical actor, this people that the historian greets as the genuine actor of the Revolution. Now, the narrative will be organized quite otherwise. It is, on the contrary, the historian who is going to appear on the stage, show himself to us, holding in his hand those narratives of federations that are much more than narratives, he tells us—they are love letters to the youthful native land: "I have found all that entire and glowing, as though made yesterday, when, sixty years afterwards, I lately opened those papers, which few persons had read."[6]

At first the historian seems to remain in the background to let the new actor speak. But, on the contrary, it is the historian who comes to the front of the stage. He has just attested that he has committed an unusual act: he has opened the cabinet of treasures and read those forgotten, sleeping testimonies. And he tells us what they are, love letters. "It is evidently the language of the heart." But this visibility of speech is only for him. What he shows to us is just what, as love letters, they make him see—not their content but their presentation. "The material details likewise gave them much solicitude: no writing seemed handsome enough, no paper elegant enough, not to mention the sumptuous little tri-coloured ribbons to tie the papers with."[7]

What designates these narratives as love letters is not what they say. It is well known that love letters never say love. The village patriots are like the young people whom love renders or finds inexperienced. Love letters repeat stereotypes, phrases from novels, sweet words borrowed from others. Thus the historian of new love does not have a place to quote them. But he will no more rewrite them than Tacitus does Percennius's harangue. Between aristocratic rhetoric and royal-empiricism, he will define a third way, another manner of treating the speech of the other. The historian will open this third way, appropriate for democratic historical knowledge, by starting with two operations of modest appearance with regard to these "love letters."

First, he makes us see them; that is, he makes himself seen to us as the one who holds them or has held them in his hand, who can attest it by the color of the ribbons, that color of the true which King Philip II could not imagine, thereby affirming himself to be inferior to the meaning that traverses him. Second, he tells us what they say: not their content but the power that causes them to be written, that is expressed in them. The historian will show us this power, which is their true content but which they are powerless to show us, by staging it in a narrative. Putting the letters whose ribbons he has shown off to us back in the closet, he will substitute a narrative for them, the narrative of the Festival. Not this one or that one, in one place or another, but the Festival in its represented essence—the country at harvest time, all the people gathered round the symbols of life, growth, and death: the newborn, a living flower among the spikes of the harvest, who cannot speak but says his civic sermon through his mother's mouth; the old man who presides, surrounded by children and with all the people as his child, the young girls, a crown of flowers or a "band . . . dressed in white," one of whom pronounces "a few noble charming sentences," of whom nothing is said to us except that they will create tomorrow's heroes.[8]

A silent old man, a child whose mother speaks for him, a virgin who harangues silently, attendants who return "lost in thought": a people whose voice is as low as that of the king of Spain. "They advance, but do not act," Michelet just told us. "Neither do they feel any necessity of acting; they advance, that is sufficient."[9] We may also say: they do not speak, they have no need to speak; they represent themselves to themselves, and that's enough. By substituting for the prolix writing of the village scholars this picture of a silent people, Michelet invents a new solution to the excess of words, to the revolution of paperwork. He invents the art of making the poor speak by keeping them silent, of making them speak as silent people.

The vanity of the humble—"eager to write, to talk of themselves and of others"—is here submitted to a very specific operation: the historian keeps them silent by making them *visible*. The narrative of the historian holding the memorials, describing the ribbons to us, and the picture of the great family celebration in the heart of the country—these ward off the disturbance of speech. They transform the *spoken*, always already spoken, always an effect and a producer of anachronism, into the *visible*. And this visible shows the meaning that speech failed to express. The truth of the narrative is founded on the reserve of meaning of the exhibited and arranged letters. But this reserve of meaning itself refers us to the real speakers: not the public writers, the village scholars, or the pedants who assume the task of composing the letters of the illiterate, but the powers of life—of birth, growth, and death—the powers of a meaning that speaks more directly in the historian's reconstituted pictures than in the overly conscientious love letters of the poor.

It is not that the speech of the "poor" is vain, that we must cleanse the words of their inexactitude to the point where the page is blank. A different assertion opposes itself to Michelet's royal-empiricism: the speakers never speak in vain. Their speech is always full of meaning. Simply put, they know nothing of the meaning that makes them speak, that speaks in them. The role of the historian is to deliver this voice. To do that, he must nullify the scene where the speech of the poor deploys its *blind* accents to lead it onto the scene of its visibility. He must lead it to quiet so that the silent voice expressed in it may speak, and so that this voice makes perceptible the real body to which it belongs. What is true of the village writer is still truer of the orator of the bigger towns. And the portrait of the great Lyonnais orator and martyr Chalier offers the best illustration of it. As with the other heroes of revolutionary eloquence, Michelet doesn't even give us the shortest phrase from this tribune's shortest declamation. That would be to place his speech outside the truth, in the logic of *mimesis*, in which the revolutionary orators imitate Tacitus imitating Percennius. Michelet quotes a single text from him: his testament, his speech, as good as dead. What is as good as dead is that the revolutionary actor speaks, lets go the voice of the life that is expressed in him. If there is no place to make Chalier speak, it is because no individual speaks through his mouth. The "extraordinary" voice of what little is left to us of his prophetic orations effectively reveals this:

> One feels it all too clearly: this prophet and holy fool is not a man like other men. What speaks is a whole city, a whole bleeding world—the agonized cry of Lyon. He is the voice of the deep dark mud of its streets, silent since the beginning of time. Through him the ancient, dismal darkness, the damp and filthy houses begin to speak; and hunger and fasts; and abandoned children and the women dishonored; and all those heaped-up, sacrificed generations. Now all these awake, now they arise, now sing from their sepulchers; and their story is of menace and death. . . . Their voices, their song, their menace, all is Chalier.[10]

The difference between the name and the word, this difference that is the burden and the delight of the homonym hunters, here finds its solution. The paradigm of republican history as Michelet founds it is that of a generalized synonymy. The name Chalier is synonymous with the voice that passes across him, synonymous with all the places and all the generations that find voice in his speech. This goes for the names of the orators as well as for the words of their orations. It is the mud of the streets, the humid and dirty houses that truly speak in the prophecies of the Lyonnais Ezekiel. In the same manner, it is the harvest, the flowers and scents of the country that are spoken in the letters of the federations—the truth of the memorial that the narrative manifests in making the report itself resemble the truth, in transforming it into a harvest flower: "These memorials of rural communes are so many wild flowers that seem to have sprung up in the midst of the harvest. In reading them we seem to inhale the strong and vivifying perfume of the country at that glowing season of fecundity. It is like walking among the ripe grain."[11]

Might we say that this rural evocation, just like that of the Lyonnais mud, belongs to the literary prehistory of historical science? That would be to remain in convenient ignorance of what literature means, in order to be in greater ignorance of what literature does here on behalf of science. The flowery metaphor is in effect quite another thing than an embellishment of the narrative. It makes the meaning of the memorials *perceptible*. And it does so in a well-defined manner. The play of sensations that it organizes among sight, smell, and touch carefully excludes one sense, that of hearing, that which lends itself to the sonorous vanity of speech. The literary metaphor identifies the "content" of the unstudied love letters with the dream of the utopia of historical study: the presence of the present, presence in the present. This metaphor sets the poetic figures of the discourse of historical study that later constitute the articulation of the Braudelian narrative. It institutes the interchangeability between the signs and privileges of narrative and those of discourse. It is Michelet, then, who conducts the revolution by which the narrative of the event becomes the narrative of its meaning. He does so in an exemplary fashion in the historian's exhibition, holding the letters and at once assuming the task of telling us not their content but the meaning of their content; *telling* us this meaning instead of producing it as the *explication* of the content of the narratives. The discourse of the scholar becomes a narrative ("I have found all that entire and glowing, as though made yesterday") so that the narrative may become a discourse, so that its autonomous unfolding—the unfolding where, says Benveniste, "no one speaks"—may hold, in the same register, the evocation of the past event ("The president at first is some old man. . . . This lovely band marches dressed in white")[12] and the explication of its meaning ("All the old emblems grow pale. . . . The true symbol is elsewhere. . . . This symbol for man is man"),[13] so that it may put them in the same present, that of the meaning present at the event ("All that *now* grows faint, or disappears").[14]

The interchangeability of the author's presence in his discourse and his absence in the autonomy of the narrative unfolding is embedded in the present in this founding narrative-discourse. Michelet is the initiator of this revolution in the system of tenses that characterizes the writing of the new history. Not that he abandons, for his part, the uses and narrative prestige of the preterit (*passé simple*). But he breaks the system of oppositions that opposed it to the present of declarations, commentaries, or maxims. He effaces it imperceptibly to the advantage of the present, so as to mark the immanence of meaning in the event. The narrative of the Festival of Unity itself presents a remarkable intersection of tenses. The historian at first seems to assume the task of marking the past ("I have found all that") to make the festival more present in its essence ("All the old emblems grow pale. . . . The president at first is some old man"). As a result, the narrative slips into the preterit (*passé simple*) in order to give its references ("At Saint-Andéol, the honour of taking the oath ... was conferred on two patriarchs").[15] He comes back to the present to impose the power of the event ("This lovely band marches dressed in white"), to make its actors familiar ("The reason is, they have to work tomorrow"),[16] or to draw lessons from the history ("Women are kept back from public life; and people are too apt to forget that they really have more right to it than any").[17] He sets himself in the imperfect to essentialize the scene ("And in fact it was in the open country that all this took place").[18] Finally he abolishes every temporal mark in order to absolutize, in a nominal phrase, the meaning of the event ("No conventional symbol! All nature, all mind, all truth!").[19]

All truth, then, where the distinctions of tense, mode, and person disappear, the distinctions that place the truth in question by relativizing the event or the position of the narrator. The nominal phrase that Michelet tears from its traditional usage—the timelessness of the maxim—so as to make it punctuate the time of the history, is not a simple effect of personal style. If Lucien Febvre piously conserved it and transmitted it to the *Annales*, he did so because it defines an essential poetic structure of the new historical knowledge. It is not simply the convenient interconnector of the tenses of discourse and those of narrative. It is, much more profoundly, the neutralization of the *appearance of the past*. This appearance is the historian's cross to bear, what motivates his desperate recourse to the "contemporary sociologist." The appearance of the past takes on what is said of nontruth: uncertainty, death, inessentiality. The nominal phrase effaces this nontruth. It is a narration without a past and an affirmation without a subject. Every indicator of distance, every mark of suspicion, putting the event at a distance or its narrator into perspective, collapses into it. It is thereby emblematic of the style of history that Michelet invents to ward off the disturbance of the speech event and to give to history the mode of truth of which it is susceptible.

It is, then, very much a question of the truth, insofar as the truth signifies more than the exactitude of the facts and figures, the reliability of the sources, and the rigor of the inductions, insofar as the truth concerns the ontological modality to which a discourse is devoted. The mud of the cities and the flowers of the fields, which speak in place of club tribunes and village writers, sufficiently warn us of it. They place us on the terrain of the truth as it has been defined for Western thought by several of Plato's propositions and questions: the condemnation of the dead letter in the name of living speech; the question of knowing whether there is an idea of the mud. To these condemnations and aporias, Micheletist poetics brings answers that are suitable for giving the new history not merely a scientific method—even a respectability—but a status of truth. The latter provides for the mud, not the idea, for which no one has the least use, but the voice that gives it flesh and converts the dead letters of writing into their living truth. And it does so by using the means of poetry to invalidate poetic nontruth.

To understand what the linguistic exchange of the forms of discourse for those of narrative effectively means, we must recognize the settlement of an old account between philosophy and poetry. In the third book of the *Republic*, Plato classed the diverse poetic forms according to their degree of falsity. This falsity increased for him the more the poet hid his own intervention behind the imitation of his characters. The least deceptive poetry was that in which the poet kept his distance from the characters, allowed himself to be seen as the speaking subject of his poem. It was that in which the mode of narrative, of *diegesis*, dominated. The most deceptive, on the other hand, was that in which the *I* of the poet and the agency of the narrative were absent. What then triumphed, exemplarily on the tragic stage, was the illusion of *mimesis*. The poet acted as though the words of his own invention were those of Orestes or Agamemnon, those of characters expressing their proper names. This condemnation of tragic *mimesis* went along, in Plato, with that of democracy. The tragic illusion itself belonged to the democratic reign of appearance and flattery, in which the arbitrariness of the orator and that of the *demos* reflected each other interminably.

If the joint condemnation of poets and democracy has been sufficiently commented on, perhaps there hasn't been enough attention given to the manner in which it is modulated, in the opposition of *mimesis* and *diegesis*, of imitation and narrative. The importance of this modulation is that it outlines the conditions of a possible redemption of poetry. By using its antimimetic powers, wouldn't narrative be suitable to offer poetry a regime of truth? And why not the same for democracy? Now it is just such a use that Michelet invents—Michelet the democrat concerned with converting democracy into truth, with removing it from the prestiges of rhetoric and the violence of tragedy. He uses the powers of narrative to destroy the system of *mimesis*, this play of mirrors of belles lettres and politics in which Tacitus, who imitated Percennius, was in turn imitated by every subsequent Percennius. *Mimesis* didn't only define the old canons of belles lettres. It was also the weapon that the Latinists and orators of the people cheaply obtained from those canons, the principle of all those peoples of the theater who give the king a bad death: a regicidal and not a republican death, rhetorical and not scientific. Destroying the primacy of *mimesis* was the requirement that had to be met by both democracy, in order to tear itself from the reign of excessive speech, and the history of the deep life of the masses, in order to succeed royal chronicles. It is what the founding narrative effects. It causes the "speech of the poor" to pass from one regime of meaning to another, to the one in which the voice of the people is no longer that of the orators. For the quotation marks that would give speech to a people of the theater, repeating the stereotypes of love for one's country, Michelet substitutes a narrative, the narrative of the love not spoken by any love letter: an antimimetic narrative. The narrative removes the spoken words from the voice of *mimesis* to give them another voice. It places their meaning on the side, in reserve, under the shelter of new imitations and new turns of language. By making the mud or the harvests speak in place of the orators and writers of the people, he gives a common root to the political reign of the people and their scholarly history, in their proper place. He gives a body to this place so that the voice of this body will pacify their turmoil. He puts in place the subject of democracy and at the same time the object of science.

Historical science doesn't win against the temptations of *narrative* and literature; it wins by the involvement of *mimesis* in narrative. It doesn't win in spite of the excesses of romanticism; it wins in the very heart of the movement called romanticism, which first of all signifies the end of the mimetic reign and the transformation of the rules of belles lettres into the unconditioned of literature.[20] In affirming itself in its absoluteness, in unbinding itself from *mimesis* and the division of genres, literature makes history possible as a discourse of the truth. It does this by the invention of a new narrative. By assuring the shift of tenses and persons into the present of meaning, this narrative founds much more than the elegance of a style.

It fixes the way of being that is suited both to the people and to science. Literature gives its status of truth to the paperwork of the poor. It suppresses and maintains at the same time, it neutralizes by its own means the condition that makes history possible and historical science impossible: the unhappy property that the human being has of being a literary animal.

This *literariness* of the historical actor is neutralized by the twofold narrative that the letters effect and that makes them disappear in the picture of what they express. This literary device of substitution furnishes a response to the question of how one in truth speaks of the revolution of the children of the Book, marks the removal of the paperwork of the poor in its truth, without this removal being the simple nonplace of the word confronted with the thing. The answer is given in the twofold narrative that, invalidating the letter, transforms it into a reserve of meaning and makes this meaning visible. Each of the two narratives then defines a position of knowledge in the face of an ignorance: the knowledge, facing the reader or the student, of the researcher who has opened the closet; the knowledge, facing inexpert speakers, of the scholar who arranges the letters in the closet to say what, in their prose, was expressed, even though she doesn't know. The play of the hidden and the visible, by which science manifests itself as such, is instituted in the gap of this twofold ignorance.

There is no science, we have learned, but that of the hidden. And the production of this *hidden* is a poetic operation essential to the constitution of knowledge in historical study. Again we must understand it, and not yield to the populist imagery that would show us the historian hiding the letters and closing the closet to assure her scholarly privilege by stripping the suffering and creative people of their knowledge and their voice. To arrange the love letters, which always say what they mean poorly, is to remove not the living flesh of the people but on the contrary their absence of flesh. It is to remove the absence or the betrayal that is at the heart of the most sincere love letter: the betrayal consisting simply of the fact that, behind the words, there is never anything but words, an absence that literature, according to the use of its powers, exposes or dissimulates.

To understand this, it is best to compare Michelet's narrative with another literary practice exhibited in other love letters addressed by illiterate persons to the revolutionary government. In the series of short narratives that form the framework of *Red Cavalry*, Isaac Babel inserts letters supposedly written by the Cossacks of the Kuban, now converted into soldiers of the Revolution on the Polish front. The intellectual enlisted in the red cavalry then imitates the love letters written by true Cossacks for the benefit of the Soviet homeland. But, of course, the Cossacks of the Kuban are incapable of writing these letters, of stating their love. And their prose can do no better than string together, with regular formulas, the stereotypes of Soviet lyricism. The true Cossacks, whose turgid speech the novelist imitates, in their turn imitate the editorials of their newspaper, the one to which they send their letters, *The Red Cavalryman*. But who then can edit these editorials except the intellectual of the company, the Jewish writer Isaac Babel or someone like him? A perfect circle of *mimesis* where a double suspicion is nurtured: a literary one—who speaks?—and a political one—who really loves, and not with words, the Soviet homeland? Never will this love manage to be stated in the native speech of the Cossacks. Never will Isaac Babel bring the odor of the steppes of the Kuban to be smelled. Behind the words of love, there is neither black mud nor a flowery village. There is nothing but betrayal and death, the death that Budenny's Cossacks will meet, that which will come to the traitor Isaac Babel, incapable of finding the words to describe and exalt the new life.

It is this betrayal or absence that closes the Micheletist narrative. Although Chalier may well be a false Lyonnais, a foreigner born in the kingdom of Piedmont, there is, behind his name and his words, everything that the militant Soviet writer and his heroes lack. There are the snows of Savoy and the roads of the pilgrims, there are the voice of the streets and that of previous generations. By arranging the letters, Michelet puts the absence away. He gives a body to the people for democracy and for science. His literary operation closes the door to literature, in the usual sense—to the vanity of words that are nothing but words. The play of the hidden letter assures that the words are never "nothing but words." There are no words without a body, no names of nothing or of no one. To the infinite resentment toward the deceptiveness of homonyms, one may oppose the general reign of synonymy—as soon as one gives to the words not their referent, which is always a risk, but the voice by which they have a body. The double narrative ensures the object of history against any betrayal of the words by staging a double authority: the authority of the scholar, of the man of the archives who stands at the source of science and transforms the ever-deceptive letter into an exact reserve of knowledge; but also the authority of that new partner that the scholar causes to speak by keeping her quiet, the *silent witness*.

The substitution of narrative for *mimesis* in effect creates this character of the silent witness, essential for the position of history as a science. This creation is nowhere summed up better than in a few lines, with a "rhetorical" appearance, of *Les Origines du droit français*. Presenting law beginning with what romanticism posits as its true origin, not property but filiation, Michelet encounters the ancient practice of the exposure of infants: a history of abandoned children that evokes not only the cruelties of the customs of antiquity but also the great founding narratives of our thought, the stories of Moses and Oedipus. Now, Michelet first brushes aside this material or symbolic cruelty. There is never, he tells us, a genuinely abandoned child. Every child is sheltered in the maternity of nature: "Cast out by man, delivered to nature, the child was often at home there. The hearty mother nature adopted him, spread leaves for him on her cold bed; she sheltered him from the north wind, fed him with wolves' milk and with the marrow of lions." No abandoned child, then. But what is essential, for us, is said in the sentences that follow, which give this proposition its equivalent in the order of meaning: there is no grief that doesn't find a voice. Every lost word is replaced by a voice that manifests its meaning: "What were the mothers' griefs? They alone could say. The stones wept over it. The ocean itself was moved when it heard the Danaë of Simonides."[21]

Here, in two sentences, the two operations that define the revolution in the discourse of historical study are summed up: a placing of speech in reserve, and a displacement of the body of speech. A placing of speech in reserve: they alone—the mothers whose voices are lost—*would be able to* say it. The conditional here introduces the figure of a paralepsis. This is the exact inverse of what paralepsis is in the rhetorical tradition: an unmentionable *mimesis*. Paralepsis fraudulently represents what it is not admissible to represent:

I could request that it be offered to your eyes
That rare and great feat of a victorious arm

In contrast to the refused presentation, the conditional here has an effect of removal: an antirhetorical, antimimetic effect. The conditional places the moaning of the mothers—that moaning that poetry has in fact never stopped imitating—in the order of the inimitable. She who alone would be able to speak the grief is absent, silent, the same distance from any imitation as the celestial constellation of Canis Major is from any barking animal. Placed under the sign of the inimitable, the content of the narration receives from her the mark of the true. The subject that one cannot imitate becomes the guarantor of the true, the witness to the occurrence of the spoken word, henceforth silent, to be made to speak anew in a discourse radically other than that of *mimesis*. The impossibility of imitation produces the silent witness who holds the truth of science, who holds this truth without herself having the power to deliver it. The figure of the one who would speak—the legitimating agency of the narration—becomes that of the silent witness—the legitimating agency of knowledge.

What is required for this is simply a displacement of the body of the voice—that which will make the Dauphinois village or the Lyonnais mud speak but which is expressed, here, as if at its zero-degree: "The stones wept over it. The ocean itself was moved when it heard the Danaë of Simonides." For the mother, who alone would be able to speak, for the inimitable mother, a discourse has just echoed, has just been substituted, a discourse of what is not in the habit of speaking, that of the place and the things. The stones cried, the ocean was moved. There is a maternal place of the speech that speaks for the silent mother. There is the ocean that protects and gives passage to Danaë, her son, and her voice.[22]

Is this pure literature, these two lines that make paper stones and an ocean of poetry cry? How could we not, nevertheless, be struck by their kinship with serious statements from serious historians? "We historians approach him rudely: he receives us as he did his ambassadors, with the utmost courtesy . . . ," or "Robespierre's death takes us from Cochin to Tocqueville"? If we understand these phrases immediately, in the implausibility of what they relate and the clarity of what they mean, isn't it by reason of the initial excess by which Michelet creates the particular regime of their signifiance?[23] This initial excess is that of a phrase that creates for history a place of truth through a narrative—or a myth—that itself is not assignable in terms of truth or falsity.

There are, then, three ways of treating myth. There is that of Simonides the poet: from tradition he receives the story of Danaë, shut up in a box by her father and delivered this way to the waves with her son, Perseus. Simonides devotes himself, in this framework, to imitating the moans of Danaë. There is the way of the mythologists who interpret these mythical stories and seek to isolate their substantial core. The latter may be, in the manner of the allegorists, a deep truth hidden under the clothing of a fable. It may be, in the critical manner, the expression of a primal sentiment: such astonishment or such basic terror of humanity figures in the originary language of fabulation. Michelet's master, Vico, for example, proceeds in this way when he explains to us the birth of Zeus in the Hellenic imagination. He shows us the archaic Greeks, struck with stupor and dread by the phenomenon of lightning and attributing its cause to a god who they assume speaks to them through these signs.[24]

Now, Michelet proceeds in a third way. He doesn't repeat, like the poets, the moans of Danaë. He doesn't wonder, like the mythologists, what the Greek fables on the loves of Zeus could have meant. Romantic writing, what makes the new history possible, is from the outset situated beyond the classical alternatives of mimetic naïveté and interpretive science. These always supposed an exteriority: that of the model one imitates or of the meaning hidden beneath the fable. Michelet, however, installs himself in the continuity of the narration that excludes the two figures of exteriority, imitation and interpretation. There would be no sense in wondering if Michelet believes the story of Danaë; no more in wondering why he includes in his demonstration a story he doesn't believe. The narration is the active liquidation of these questions. It proves just by itself, in its continuity that suspends all question of belief, that there is no exteriority in relation to meaning, no nonsense. The narration establishes that nonsense cannot be. It speaks the immanence of meaning—of the same meaning for everything that is said. Everything speaks according to the same modality: the displacement from sonorous speech to the voice of the silent witness. The narrative of the stones and the ocean that cry gives history its founding mythology. And *mythology* must be understood outside of any pantheonesque reference and any phantasmagoria of archetypes. *Mythology* here means, very precisely, *discourse-narrative*, the equivalence of narrative and discourse: the *muthos* that is a *logos*, the narrative that produces reason, the science that is given in the form of narrative. The primary *muthos* of the accompanied voyage of Danaë and Perseus is the very narrative of the *logos*. The defining feature of the *logos*, according to the romantic etymology of the Greek *legein*, is that it gathers: it brings to every child its mother, to every grief its voice, to every voice its body; it leads every word, like every mother, intact, in the security of the narration inhabited by its meaning, of the narration that leaves no place for non-sense. Literature must show, against itself, this defining feature of the *logos*. The Danaë of Simonides—the poet, the liar—is a fiction. But from the poetic tissue, one can extract what Simonides does not say: those sobs of the sea and the stones. One can make them true, make them pass over to the side of truth. The side of truth is where the spoken words are no longer written on paper or on the wind, but engraved in the texture of things. It is the place of an expressivity and a signifiance that are opposed to those words of chatterers always contaminated by the lie of *mimesis*. The *truth*, Michelet tells us, is better read in cries than in spoken words, better in the disposition of things than in the ordering of discourse. It is better read where no one is trying to speak, where no one is trying to deceive. The theory of the silent witness ties two statements that are at first sight contradictory. First, everything speaks, there is no silence, no lost speech. Second, the only one who speaks is the one who is silent.

"Guardian of the earth, man's monument, the tomb contains a silent witness who would speak as needed."[25] Rather than be amused with this "necromantic" phantasm of Michelet, we must recognize the figure of the logical structure on which he builds his images: the only one who speaks is the one who *would speak*. And not, certainly not, the one who *spoke*. The conditional—the anti-imperfect—of speech in reserve, of speech in the tomb, can alone found the present without the falsity of the narrative of historical study. The only one who speaks is *the only one who would be able to speak*. The silent voice of the conditional is that which can come back to us only through the tombstone or the cries of the rocks: a voice without paper, a meaning indelibly inscribed in things, which one may read, which one *would be able* to read endlessly in the materiality of the objects of everyday life. "One *would have* to be able here to enumerate all the silent signs by which man has recounted and repeated to himself this delightful mystery: symbols of clothing that recall with a chaste sexuality the confusion of two existences; symbols of domestic occupation that express the harmonious diversity of labors; symbols of the household that promise gentle company throughout one's life."[26] Here, with marriage, as before with filiation or death, there is a little more pathos than our positive ears can bear. But our construction sites of history are opened by those symbols of works and days, those histories of kinship and household, of stones and death. And what opens this conditional that makes them present is the condition of the new writing in historical study: the symbolic order of which the silent witness is the chaste or dead guardian.

It is, then, this world of silent witnesses that the historian brings into a significance without lies, that history in our century will reclaim as its realm—in place of ambassadors' letters or of the paperwork of the poor, the multiplicity of spoken words that do not speak, of messages inscribed in things. Michelet's "romantic" excess is only the excess of the foundation, of the symbolic order that makes possible the decipherings of a more sober history: the deciphering of those territories in which we will read the character, action, and constraints of those which they have produced and which have transformed them in return; the deciphering of all the monuments and all the traces of what we call material civilization—the world of objects and tools, the practices of the everyday, the uses of the body, and the symbolic behaviors; the entire domain, in short, of the great regularities of material life and of the slow mutations of history and of mentalities that Michelet, the at once honored and burdensome father of our scholarly history, opened for it. If our century has been able to oppose the solidity of this universe to the vanity of letters but also to the romantic verbiage of the author of the *Histoire de France*, it is because he initially marked this realm as the space of an *everything speaks*, because he marked the folds of the territory or the erosion of the stones, the household objects, or the gestures of everyday life as the scene of an uninterrupted discourse, because he instituted them as silent witnesses, bearers of an inscription and a message. He made these into the detached fragments of a configuration of meaning that is constituted through reassembly, of a symbolic meaning, in the originary sense of *sumbolon*: the object broken in two whose pieces, reunited, bear witness to the union.

The primary union among all things is the union of body and voice, that is, ultimately, the union of mother and child, of the maternal agency of meaning and the filial and masculine agency of discourse. It is very precisely this logic of sense that relates the accompanied voyage of Danaë and her son. This child, carried intact with his mother by the ocean, has a celebrated name in mythology. It is Perseus, the victor over the Medusa with the petrifying face, the hero who frees Andromeda and her mother, the hero who frees woman in general, who frees the maternity of meaning that first carried him and that he must subsequently deliver from the stone that holds her. To the book of abandoned, sheltered, and patricidal children, Michelet in fact adds a singular page. He puts a younger brother to Oedipus and Moses on the scene. If Perseus is shut up in a box with his mother, it is because the oracle predicted to his grandfather Acrisius that his daughter's son would kill him. Whence Acrisius's precautions, as well as what follows: Danaë imprisoned in her turn, visited by the golden rain, and in punishment delivered to the waves with her son. But Perseus is a happy Oedipus. Far from marrying his mother, he rescues her from an unworthy husband. And he will kill his grandfather only by chance in a stadium accident. The myth of Perseus thus offers the most optimistic version of the wound of the speaking subject: the child who is sheltered, as soon as he is abandoned, in the maternity of nature and meaning, and who pays his debt exactly by freeing his mother and the mother nature that carried him—the earthly matrix by which there is speech and meaning, even if this meaning is only in its turn raised up and freed by the child that it carried.

We know that this poetic myth of history is, indissolubly for Michelet, a political myth. The theory of the symbol strictly holds together the three contracts—the narrative, the scientific, and the political—of the historian. What must succeed the genealogies and emblems of royalty is a new way of thinking about the transmission of meaning and about legitimate descent, a new relation between the filiation of bodies and the order of discourse. For democratic politics and the scholarly historical narrative, Michelet invents this new way of thinking about the filiation between the maternal and poetic order of nature, on the one hand, and the masculine order of sober science and of the republic of law, on the other. He invents the symbolic order in which a movement must be deployed that is at once one of progress and one of return. Man is his own Prometheus. He is the statue that extracts itself from the marble, the son that tears himself from the primary feminine universe of nature and grace. But this movement from grace to justice, from primary symbolism to the rational order, is possible only through the movement of return that reestablishes the filiation that is always threatened with its own loss. The son must recognize his primary bond, his debt toward the earthly and maternal origin of common meaning, in order better to transfigure it into the austere equilibria of reason and justice. The labor of the historian, in the modern republic, is the settlement of this debt, the reestablishment of that bond between the republic of law and its original land. Because of that, the historian must begin by returning to the source, by once again becoming a child to understand the state of *in-fancy*, in the sense of not speaking, inscribed in the texture of things. Only at this price is it possible to unite the republic to its soil and its past, the scholars and politicians to their people.

Assuredly, we are far from these maternal legends and filial duties. But the legitimate irritation of the serious historian with regard to these childish pursuits may be read in the wrong way. The positive fortune of the social sciences is also what is left to us of a lost political utopia. The dream of Michelet, like that of Comte or Durkheim, of Mauss or Lucien Febvre, has managed to disappear. What remains is that the fable of Danaë and Perseus best represents the new regime of meaning, the new symbolic order in which scholarly history can find its language and syntax, between the dead chronicles of the sovereigns and the intrusive chatter of the poor.

The Place of Speech

In order to be calmed, the disturbance of the paperwork of the poor, this disturbance that invades lost time and puts history outside truth, thus requires a determinate theory of the relations between the order of discourse and the order of bodies; a determinate theory of the speaking subject, of the relations between the subject, knowledge, speech, and death. It assumes, in short, a certain idea of the unconscious and a certain practice of psychoanalysis.

This idea can be represented in the myth of Perseus, Oedipus's younger, happier brother. But the Oedipus that Michelet knows is himself a happy hero who doesn't pose a threat of either incest or patricide. Contrary to Sophocles' hero, the only fault he could commit would be to fail in his duty of searching, no longer to be concerned with his parents. It would be to lapse in his mission, which is to free captive maternal meaning, to wrest it from its petrifaction. No death at the end of the decipherment. The enigma, on the other hand, is only of the death that he must bring to life. The historian is an Oedipus. And Oedipus is himself a psychoanalyst, in the literal sense: a liberator of souls. We must understand *souls* in the ancient sense: the souls to be delivered are the inhabitants of Hell who groan over their shadowy condition and sigh for the blood of earthly life. Happier than voyagers like Ulysses or Aeneas, the historian has the power to bring

61

them to life. For he knows the secret of their death, the secret that he sums up in a tiny and decisive shift of meaning: the dead souls of Hell are those of individuals who died *too early to know* what they had lived, who died *in order not to have known soon enough* what it means to live, in order not to have known how to say it. Michelet lends them his pen so that they may themselves confess the secret of their death, which is that they were not familiar with the enigma of life: "We died, still stammering. Our pitiful chronicles confirm that enough. We did not realize mankind's sovereign attribute, the distinct, clear voice that alone explains, consoles by explaining. . . . And if we had had a voice, could we have expressed life? We did not know how."[1]

"We died, still stammering": the suspension produced by a participle renders a temporal as well as a causal relation indiscernible. Life dies from the stammering of life, from life's delay in being known and stated. The anachronistic turmoil of voices that causes the disturbance in politics and knowledge amounts to that essential anachronism in the destiny of the speaker, to the fact that living implies not knowing what life is, that speaking implies not knowing what one is saying. The unconscious is just the lack of this knowledge of life that is inherent in the living being seized by speech. And death is itself only another name for this non-knowledge. The unconscious and death are two equivalent notions, the one substitutable for the other. To be dead is not to know, to be waiting for the liberating knowledge of oneself. To calm the turmoil of the voices is to calm death, to appease the crowd of those who have died from not knowing and not knowing how to say what it means to live. To free the souls—the dead—from this ignorance, what is sufficient, then, is an Oedipus as psychoanalyst who tells them their secret:

> They need an Oedipus who will solve their own riddles, whose meaning they do not know, who will teach them what their words, their acts—which they do not understand—signify. They need a Prometheus. And when he has stolen the fire, the icy voices that float in the air will come together, produce sounds, begin speaking again. We need more. We must hear the words that were never spoken. . . . We must make the silences of history speak, those fearsome organ pauses when history speaks no more and which are precisely its most tragic tones.

Only then do the dead accept the sepulcher. They begin to understand their destiny and gather its agonizing distances into a softer harmony, to say to each other, very quietly, Oedipus's final words: *pántos gàr ékhei táde kûros* [Everything has been fulfilled]. The shades are soothed and appeased. They allow their urns to be closed again.[2]

There are two ways of reading this passage from Michelet's journal. We can see in it the marks of time and of the obsessions of a man. We then recognize in it the child who enjoyed himself in the cemeteries, the widower who has the body of his wife unearthed so that he may observe it, the scientist, assiduous about his medical school colleagues' dissections. We thus follow the direct route that goes from this necrophilic obsession to the privilege of being dead that the historian himself claims, to cross and recross the river of the dead, "so many times," to retire the debt of history to those who call him back: "We accepted death for one line of you."[3] But we can also take things another way, beginning with this line of writing that is itself suspended by the necessity of the river that is crossed and recrossed. The "necrophilic phantasm" will then appear as the element of a rigorous theoretical framework. The identification of death and the unconscious is the inclusion of death in science, not as a residue but as a condition of possibility. The constitution of history as a discourse of truth requires the possibility of positively tying together the twofold absence that is at the heart of historical affect. There is history because there is a past and a specific passion for the past. And there is history because there is an absence of things in words, of the denominated in names. The status of history depends on the treatment of this twofold absence of the "thing itself" that is *no longer there*—that is in the past; and that never was—because it never was *such as it was told*. Historical affect is bound to the personal absence of what the names name.

It is in relation to this absence that the positions of historical discourse are defined. Revisionism assimilates the condition of possibility of history to its condition of impossibility. It dramatizes the twofold absence by which there is history in the figure of the murderous words and of the regicide where any proportion between words and things collapses. But Michelet makes the equivalence function the other way around: the condition of impossibility of history is none other than its condition of possibility. Each of its forms of absence is none other than the other. Death is only the non-knowledge of the living. The deceptiveness of words is only the transitory necessity of death. The twofold absence is a twofold reserve of a presence: of a life to revive and of a knowledge that affirms itself by the very death that its lack brings about. Every catastrophe of politics and knowledge is abolished in this equivalence of ignorance and death that the historian—the son, the survivor—quite naturally quells: by adding to past life, ignorant of itself, the knowledge—the supplement of life—that its sum lacked; but also, on the other hand, by giving the discourse of history the dimension of absence and concealment that alone lifts it out of the platitude of chronicling. The redemption of absence is needed for history to be separated from novelistic treachery. But a *contract* with absence, the inclusion of death, is needed for it to be separated from the old tradition of chronicling.

This is, effectively, the flaw in the very principle of chronicle-based history. It isn't science or number that causes it to be afraid, but death. It pretends to make work of positive method and science by refusing the "embodied abstractions," by sticking to the subjects and events that indisputable documents are capable of attesting. But the secret of this false rigor is the fear of death. Chronicle-based history has no fetishistic attachment to the deeds and gestures of kings and their ambassadors. Its adherents are good republicans. It is much more attached to the continuity of life and of the institution in which a king succeeds the dead king and names an ambassador in place of another. Positivist history refuses to confront the absence of its object, that "hidden" without which there is no science and which can't be reduced to the archive buried in its files. This "hidden" that Michelet gives to historical science is life hidden from death. But chronicle-based history remains stuck to this stammering life. All it can do, then, is stammer with it or fill in the holes that allow it to rationalize its stammering. In the "historical method" of Seignobos, this rationalization has a significant name. It is called psychology. "Psychology" allows the historian to tighten the thread between the documents.[4] But what then is this psychology? Precisely that "science of the soul" of those who are afraid of death, who refuse the liberating descent into Hell, the identification of the soul with death.

Revisionist demonology, however, puts death at the center of its argument, but under a very precise figure. It suspends itself at the scandal of regicide that is the death of legitimacy imputable to the falsity of words. It congeals death in a Medusa's head and constitutes itself, from that point on, as an interminable denunciation of ideology. But the denunciation of ideology is not science. It is only the vague desire for science, which consumes itself in resentment toward deceptive powers. The becoming-science of the historical narrative is beyond the alternative between forgotten death and petrified death. It passes through that "mythological" confrontation that at once includes and suppresses death. The inclusion of death is the identification of the past and the unconscious—of the not-yet conscious—that transforms the "falsity" of words and that of the past into a reserve of presence and knowledge. The silent witness of the tomb is strictly identical to the "hidden" required by science. The "voice" of the tomb figures quite well, beyond all necrophilic phantasm, a precise rationality, that of the new historical science. The chatterers' voice without place—those chatterers who are dead from not knowing what they were saying—is redeemed as the voice of the silent witness, the voice legitimated by the place that gives it a place and passage. The tomb is death redeemed from its falsity, death insofar as it has its place and gives a place. The "passion" of the tomb can be reduced to the sobriety of the logical game by which the productions of the speaker are treated for every bite that absence has given them. Everything speaks, everything has a meaning, to the degree that every speech production is assignable to the legitimate expression of a place: the earth that shapes men, the sea on which their exchanges take place, the everyday objects in which their relations can be read, the stone that retains their imprint. The inclusion of death and the theory of the silent witness are one and the same theory: a theory of the place of speech.

It is in this definition of a place of speech that a way of thinking about the tomb and a way of thinking about the ground are tied together; a theory of death as the passage of voices and a theory of space as an inscription of meaning. Without this articulation, we would poorly understand the twofold preoccupation that never stops guiding the directions of research in the new history to the apparently distant territories of geography and religion. How do we conceive the necessity that requires Lucien Febvre to go from *A Geographical Introduction to History* to *Rabelais and the Problem of Unbelief*, Marc Bloch from *French Rural History* to *Sacred Monarchy and Scrofula*, or Emmanuel Le Roy Ladurie from *Histoire du climat depuis l'an mil* to the study of the Catharism of Montaillou? We know that Lucien Febvre emphasized the debt of the new history to human geography. And he honored that debt with a work destined to clear the geographers and the historians who emulated them of the grievance of "geographic determinism" uttered by the Durkheimian sociological school. *A Geographical Introduction to History* tries to trace a middle path between the antigeographicism of the sociologists and the excess of the anthropo-geography of Ratzel. But this combat on the front of causes and laws, inherited from the scientistic age, leaves in shadow what more profoundly links the new historical project to a geographic paradigm. The "geographicization" of history in fact goes back to Michelet, and it doesn't seek to arm history with a theory of causes. Its effect would instead be, on the contrary, to permit history to escape the great scientistic battle of laws and causes. The geographic "basis" that Michelet gives history, even if it is a response to the theory of races, is not the submission of historical facts to geographic data. It is, much more profoundly, a geographicization or a territorialization of meaning. It is not a question of the influence of the ground or milieu. The ground specifically doesn't go without the tomb. The ground is an inscription of meaning, the tomb a passage of voices. The "geography" to which the new history appeals is first of all a symbolic space that gives the kings a good death and establishes the first condition of historical science: that no spoken word is left without a place. History can be republican and scholarly through the invention of a certain psycho-analysis: of a freeing of the souls that itself rests on a certain unconscious, a geography of the symbolic. It is republican and scholarly through the "romantic" operation of a territorialization of meaning. The latter distributes the excess of words and the division of voices between the earth and the sea, between plains and mountains, islands and peninsulas. The republican death of the king takes place, in Michelet, to the advantage of a people without a paperwork of their poor, that territorialized people portrayed in *Le Tableau de la France*: a mosaic of men descending from some mountain, emerging from some grove, working some plain, reflecting some sky, or blanketed by fog. The Micheletist theory of place removes the possibility that any spoken word would ever be vain. It prohibits nonsense by making of every speech production the exact expression of its cause. The children of the Book would thus never get lost. For the phrases of every book are, ultimately, the voices of territorialized bodies shaped by the character of a land. It is not a matter of geologic determinism. The fancies of the disciples of Taine will demonstrate it *a contrario*: any place at all lends itself to engendering any character at all. It is much more a matter of the putting into play of a principle of generalized expressivity, of transitivity from writing to the voice, from the voice to the body, from the body to the place. It is a matter, finally, of the play of a single amphibology: *the place is what gives a place*. All speech production can be represented as the exact expression of what gives it a place, of its own legitimacy. Thus the discourse of the book, as utopian or heterodox as it appears, is always interpretable as a *doxa*, as the expression of a *topos*.

We can state it otherwise: there is no possible *heresy*. And here we can grasp the necessity that links the territorial thought of the new history to the question of religious dissidence. We know that the latter figured among the major preoccupations of the historians of the age of the *Annales*: the problematic unbelief of Rabelais, the Catharism of the peasants and shepherds of Montaillou, the heresy of Menocchio the miller, among many others. And we may at first be surprised that religion and its deviations preoccupied those historians so much. How do we comprehend that Lucien Febvre sorted out, for ten years, clerics' petty quarrels, forgotten in old papers, to establish, in sum, that Rabelais only had and only could have had the religion of his century? The very disproportion between this passionate engagement and the new scale of historical greatness seems to indicate the following: heresy is not a particular object of the history of mentalities. It poses, rather, the question of the very possibility of such a history. The history of mentalities is possible insofar as heresy is put back in its place, assigned to its time and place. For heresy is the very essence of what the paperwork of the poor and the revolution of the children of the Book manifest. It is the excess of speech, the violence that comes through the book, about the book. If heresy tears apart the social body for questions of words, it is because it is first of all the very disturbance of the speaker: the disturbance of life seized by writing, of the life that is separated from itself, that turns against itself because of writing. Heresy is the life of meaning, inasmuch as it resists all play of nature and of its symbolization, as it always falls prey to that excess or flaw that Michel de Certeau, in *The Mystic Fable*, analyzes exemplarily: on the one hand, the excess of speech that doesn't find its place, illustrated by the erratic destiny of the priest Labadie, at one time or another a Jesuit, Calvinist, Pietist, chiliast, and finally—a mortal step for homonymy—a Labadist;[5] on the other, the radical flaw of a life rendered silent by the observance of the Scripture, exemplified by the "madwoman" of the monastery of Tabennesi, the nameless one who disappears as soon as she is recognized.

> The madwoman, because she is never *there* where it could be spoken, has falsified the contract that the institution guarantees. . . . Ultimately no contract, not even the first and last of all contracts, language itself, is honored by her. In repeating our words and our stories, she insinuates into them their deceitfulness. Perhaps while the *sym-bolos* is a union-producing fiction, she is a *dia-bolos*, a dissuasion from the symbolic through the unnameability of that thing.[6]

Such is the stake of heresy for history. Heresy is *separation*, according to its etymology, but in a specific sense—it is, in the strict sense, *dia-bolic*: a broken *sumbolon* that can't be fixed, a piece of metal or language that can't be adjoined to any other, a motherless child, a voice separated from the body, a body separated from the place. The chatterer is without a place that takes her in, the silent witness does not speak. The agency of the diabolic forbids the exchange of bodies that causes the place of truth to speak in place of the unconscious chatterers. One could say that it forbids a history of mentalities. For the latter to be possible, it must settle its account with the devil. It must give him a place, attach him to his place. And to do that it must radically reinterpret the heretical difference, suppress the out-of-place that is identified with nonsense. The principle of this reinterpretation is simple. It reduces the diabolic to the misunderstood symbolic. It makes, of the heretical separation, the simple difference between the two places.

Here again, Michelet is the strict initiator of the revolution that founds a history of mentalities. The "most unassailable" of his books, the one he thought about for the twenty years in which he wrote his *Histoire de France, Satanism and Witchcraft*, gives it the most exact formula. It is a matter of transforming the devil, a "hollow being," into a living and signifying reality, of giving him his real name along with his living flesh. For that, according to the "filial" logic of the symbolic order, it is necessary to give him a mother. The true name of the devil is Satan, son of that "warm and living reality" stigmatized with the name of witch by the men of the Book. The "devil" is a paper creature invented by the sterile servants and imitators of the word to disembody, to diabolize Satan, the son of the witch's loyalties and dreams. And the witch is herself only woman, the primary guardian of the symbolic alliance between the body and the place, the loyal servant of the spirits of the earth and of the divinities of the home. The "witch" is only "the Church's crime,"[7] the woman unrecognized, in her function as guardian of domestic and earthly symbolism, by the government of men alone, of the worshippers of the dead book. She is the genius of the place and the hearth, of that terrestrial cult denied by the contemnors of the world. Satan is the son, the living reality of her imagination, the substitute for those divinities of the place proscribed by the Church but indestructibly living "in the most intimate of domestic habits," in the heart of the home, the bed, and the cradle. He is the soul proscribed from his home, from the place of the transmission, of the filiation of bodies and meaning. The diabolic is the denied and forbidden symbolicity of mother nature, of the place that gives a place. There is no diabolic, no interruption, and no collapse of meaning except through the operation of the men of the one Book, the sons who have forgotten their mother.

Michelet in this way sets the condition of a history of mentalities: all witchcraft or all heresy, all fancy or all silence can be reduced to its place, to be analyzed as a product of the same expressive power. The aberration of the other is never anything but the unrecognized power of the same. Anachronism and nonsense are without place. The devil is, in the strict sense, domesticated: assigned to a *domus*, transformed into the historian's familiar collaborator. Thanks to the Micheletist excess, the scholarly historian of our century can cast an amused glance at the devil's controlled pilgrimages: "The Devil seems to have been afoot in all the countries of Europe as the sixteenth century drew to a close, and even more in the first decades of the following century. He even seems to have crossed over into Spain by the high Pyrenean passes." From Michelet's fire the Devil emerges appeased, having become the cultural production whose stages and displacements are derivable from differences in place and time: "But we must leave this fascinating topic, as our chief interest for the moment is the problem of disparity between mountain and lowland, of the backwardness of mountain society."[8]

A disparity between one place and another. One time period moving more slowly than another; that is what "this fascinating topic"—the disturbance of life seized by speech—may always amount to. That is what the blood debts of religious difference are reduced to. "The root of it all was religion: isolation was the consequence of a whole complex of inherited habits, beliefs, even methods of preparing food."[9] For Braudel's robust indifferentism, the clash between the very Catholic royalty and the Jews in Spain can do without any reference to the Book or to the people of the Book. It can be sufficiently represented in the combat between lard-based cooking and oil-based cooking, in which the expulsion of the Jews is compensated by the naturalization of their cooking in a movement of attraction and repulsion, the latter constitutive of every civilization. And this necessity to "share itself," proper to a civilization, may ultimately be understood according to the model of geologic displacements: "A Christian Spain was struggling to be born. The glacier displaced by its emergence crushed the trees and houses in its path."[10] The brutality of this geologic assignation in the heart of the refinements of this history of a thousand speeds shows the stake of the question: behind the explicit project of these pages, which is to temper the overly easy charge of anti-Semitism lodged against the Spanish monarchy, there is the concern of clearing the terrain of history of the irregularities of religious war. The historian of world economies plays, without nuances, on the literal and figurative of geologic determinism, as before he played on the "weight of numbers" that culminated in the vicious circle—the demographic pressure explaining the expulsion of the Jews that served to prove this pressure.[11] But it is always, in the final analysis, a theory of the genius of the place that the historian who is more attentive to mentalities must put into play, in order to account for the war of writing that ravages the societies of speakers.

There is, for example, that singular theological controversy that is debated in the year 1318 in the highland of Ariège:

"During that year," recounts Bertrand Cordier, a native of Pamiers,
"I found, on the other side of the bridge, above the territory of the

parish of Quié, four Tarasconais, among them Arnaud de Savignan.
They asked me:
" 'What's new at Pamiers?'
" 'They say there that the Antichrist is born,' I told them, among
other things. 'So everyone must put his soul in order; the end of the
world is approaching!'
"To which Arnaud de Savignan interjected: 'I don't believe that!
The world has no beginning or end. . . . Let's go to bed.' "[12]

A speech event, if ever there was one: before the tribunal of judges
avenging infidelity to the Scripture, a witness came to report, in the past
tense, on the new things being said at Pamiers in 1318—the imminent
coming of the Antichrist and how, one day, before going to bed, a mason
of Tarascon raised an objection to it. How does one account for this speech
event? How does one account for the extravagance of this mason who
casually affirms the eternity of the world? The historian's response is quite
simply to follow the tendency of this casualness, the tendency toward
familiarity that brings all excess of speech back to its natural place, to the
place that gives flesh to its voice. The heresy of the mason of Tarascon is
not a theological subtlety; it is only the expression of a mountain dweller's
skepticism with regard to the millenarianism of those agitated cities where
they believe in the event. Doesn't he quote, in support of his theological
daring, a mischievous proverb of his land, "Always and forever, a man
will sleep with his neighbor's wife"? The eternity of the world is not a
matter of theology. It may be affirmed in the same mode of popular wis-
dom as the durability of adultery. It belongs to what is said in the mountains of Sabbarthès. It expresses the spontaneous vision of those men of
the mountains who live at great remove from the rigorous dogmas of the
changing ideas of the cities: "Sabbarthès, stuck in an avant-garde
archaism, presents itself as barely susceptible to the new (even deviating)
currents of Catholic sensibility."[13] The mountains are of necessity closer to
their heaven, which is older and newer than that of the city and dogma.
And there is no contradiction between this skepticism and the success of
Catharism. The reason that makes the mountain dwellers of Sabbarthès
skeptical also nurtures the Catharist faith in Montaillou. It is the faith of
the peasant who can imagine another world only as similar to his own,
who refuses the paradise of the theologians and the subtleties of the resur-

rection of the flesh to the benefit of a paradise structured like the peasant *domus*, animated by the heat of the *ostal*. And it is again the practical sense of the inhabitants of Montaillou that makes them adhere to the doctrine of those *purists* who take on themselves the strict observance of the commandments of purified religion and allow their lax mode of life to continue until the day of *consolamentum*. Heresy may thus be thought according to the exact adequation of meaning and place. It is the identity of a separate territory: the *identity* of a spontaneously pagan peasant universe (*paganus*, as we know, means both pagan and peasant), faithful, like Michelet's witch, to the ancient and forever young divinities of the home, the earth, and fertility; the *separation* of a mountain dweller's world that is not concerned with the doctrine of the cities until the day the latter comes to care about it.

For in what we name historical reality, of course, this distant encounter between orthodoxy and heterodoxy has taken the form of a merciless encounter between the Inquisition and heresy. And the shadow of the yellow crosses comes to fall on the living description of village society. The mischievous explanation of the advantages of the *consolamentum*, in which the ethnological sense of the historian sympathized in the present with the practical sense of the eternal peasant, then congeals in the solemnity of a greeting for the dead. "One may be tempted to say that Montaillou found the solution to the classical problem: *how to get to heaven without tiring oneself out*. But the choice that the village made on this issue, under the yellow crosses, was so heavy with inquisitorial repression, courageously assumed by the victims, that it would be indecent to present the question in such humorous terms."[14]

One may be tempted . . . ; it would be indecent. . . . Here again the paralepsis is not a mere matter of rhetoric. What it effects is a short circuit between two states of speech, two captures of the speaker by writing. There is what the document of the inquisitors delivers to the sagacity of the historian, armed with the methods of ethnology and village sociology: testimonies that allow the reconstruction of a network of social relations and its perceptible humus—a way of inhabiting a language and a land at the same time, a savor of words, a voice of the place. And there is what the document doesn't say, what it is content to be: the event of the Inquisition, this death as the price of turning away from the Scripture that breaks both the tranquility of the village mores and the tranquility of their interpretation. Of course the historian measures, in his own way, the relation of the stated to the unstated. Emmanuel Le Roy Ladurie knows that it is the "misfortune" of the villagers that gives him the "fortune" to exploit an exceptional material to reinstate the life of the "peasants of flesh and blood" of Montaillou.[15] He consequently knows what can and can't be said about that speech "given" to the villagers by the inquisitor. And he suspends the mischievous interpretation of the "low-priced heaven" of the Catharist villagers when it appears that this interpretation plays an indecent game with death. But we must understand the function of this suspension. We could at first think it is only a clause of politeness. As soon as the dead are greeted, then, the explanation once again takes up the thread of the same logic and the same playful tone ("One can therefore keep the old, charming, and lax Sabbarthesian way of life").[16] It is nevertheless not simply a matter of greeting the dead on their passing. It is a matter, in Micheletist terms, of leading them back to their tomb, of separating them from the living: of burying the heretics stricken with death so as to revive the peasants of Montaillou.

The suspension of the interpretation disconnects village sociology from the destiny of death brought by the Inquisition. In the disjunction that is thereby assured between the normally deviating life of the village and the inquisitorial death, something merely disappears, falls out of the picture: something unthinkable, heresy itself. It would be wrong to say that the historian doesn't want to know about the Inquisition. What he doesn't want to know about is heresy: life turned away from the word, turned away by the word. It would be futile to reproach him with a reductive interpretation of heresy. Specifically, his intention is not to interpret heresy, "to give an exhaustive account of the Albigeois theologies," but "to indicate, in passing, how these theologies were embodied in the flesh of the social, in the heart of a village."[17] His object is not heresy, but the village that gives it a place. But to give heresy a place is to suppress it as such, to inter it by territorializing it. The inquisitor suppresses heresy by eradicating it: he marks it, he locks it up, he kills it. The historian, on the contrary, suppresses it by giving it roots. He removes it, as it were retrospectively, from the inquisitorial condemnation by giving it the color of the earth and the stones, by rendering it indiscernible from its place.

In this way the fundamental relation between the history of mentalities and heresy becomes evident. The historian of mentalities doesn't encounter heresy as a particular section of his territory. He encounters it as the identity of the condition of possibility and the condition of impossibility of such a territory. It was necessary for there to be heresy, so that something would be written that had no reason to be: the life of an Ariégeois village during the fourteenth century. It is necessary for heresy to disappear, so that this life would be rewritten in the present of a history of mentalities. There is material for a history of mentalities *inasmuch as there is heresy*, the production of speech without a place, devoted to death. There is a history of mentalities *inasmuch as there is no heresy*, no speech that is not the expression of the life of a place, no heaven that is not the expression of an earth. The identity of the condition of possibility and the condition of impossibility functions positively by the operation that leads the dead back to their tomb. One must always begin the operation again so that the Ariégeois village of 1318, like the Dauphinois village of July 1790, begins to speak, so that the historian becomes a "contemporary" of this speech, an ethnologist of the past. The destiny of a historical discourse-narrative is suspended by the interpretation of two events, two extreme relations of the speaker with death: regicide and the Inquisition. Regicide is unredeemable death, legitimacy that has collapsed in the turmoil of voices where no silent one may be heard, only chatterers. This death without redemption determines the royal-empiricist resentment toward words up to the "revisionist" point of the breech of the contract of historical study. Inquisitorial death, on the contrary, is redeemable death, which makes the silences and the silent ones of history speak. It is why the "psychoanalysis" of the witch is the necessary detour at the foundation of a republican history, of a history freed from the Medusa's head that is the king.

Oedipus the historian can never cease to be a "necrophile" if he wants to give the blood of life to the dead souls. It is through this psychoanalysis of the dead that history, putting the scientistic compasses into a spin, accedes to the dignity of science while remaining a history. Death, calmed down, gives it the terrain where it can become an ethnology of the past. But it is also the sustained operation of leading the dead back that keeps it from disappearing in its victory, from no longer being only an ethnology or a sociology of the past. The difference proper to history is death; it is the power of death that attaches itself solely to the properties of the speaker, it is the disturbance that this power introduces into all positive knowledge. The historian can't stop effacing the line of death, but also can't stop tracing it anew. History has its own life in this alternative throbbing of death and knowledge. It is the science that becomes singular only by playing on its own condition of impossibility, by ceaselessly transforming it into a condition of possibility, but also by marking anew, as furtively, as discreetly as can be, the line of the impossible.

The Space of the Book

The *geo-history* of the space-times of material life and the *ethnohistory* of mentalities are thus elaborated around the same essential tension, in which the speech event tends to disappear in its territorialization to the point where history, so as not to disappear itself, must redraw the effaced line of union. To draw this line, which gives history its proper domain, is to mark anew the line of meaning and death: the line of historiality and literariness, without which there would be no place to write history. So, around the denied heresy, the plays of meaning between the living place and the speech of death are ordered; but perhaps also, more secretly, are the plays of the earth and sea around the fable of the dead king.

Let's return to that allegorical narrative of the event-based death and the conceptual destitution of the king, in order to understand it. Now we are doubtless better able to comprehend the meaning of this destitution: why and how the heritage of the king's "force of history" must be removed from the people of paper that encumbers his desk. In the line of the Micheletist revolution, this crowd of chatterers is replaced by the picture of a people emerged from the diversity of grounds that give them a place. They are no longer the nation-people of *Le Tableau de la France*, but a world-people: the mosaic composed, in the apparent disparity of territories and the difference of temporalities, by the Castilian carrier and the banker of Augsburg, the nomad of Arabia or the Caucasus and the Venetian shipowner, the planter of Cyprus, the sailor of Ragusa, and the Galician water merchant of Madrid. But this territorialization of the people of paper doesn't in the least exhaust the significance of the theoretical event signified by the death of the king: the displacement of the force of history from the king, from his capacity to be the center and organizer of history, to the new subject named the Mediterranean.

Let's go back, then, to the last lines of the chapter:

> I do not believe that the word Mediterranean itself ever floated in his consciousness with the meaning we now give it, nor that it conjured up for him the images of light and blue water it has for us; nor even that it signified a precise area of major problems or the setting for a clearly conceived policy. Geography in the true sense was not part of a prince's education. These are all sufficient reasons why the long agony which ended in September, 1598 was not a great event in Mediterranean history; good reasons for us to reflect once more on the distance separating event-based history from the history of structures, and even more from the history of spaces. . . .[1]

Geography in the true sense? What exactly does that mean? And how is this genuine geography in accord with those images of light and blue water that Braudel himself so often likes to oppose? What does this "even more" signify, which is not satisfied with going back over the architecture of the book, but even seems to give to the spaces the vacant crown that the structures seemed to call? And the suspension points that end the paragraph and the chapter? They are certainly not isolated in the Mediterranean. But their repetition, echoing in each paragraph of the narrative of the royal death, and the suspension they carry to the extreme edge of the book singularly dramatize the narrative and theoretical role they play throughout the book: the mimed movement of a sailor's departure for an ever-hazardous destination; that of an argument toward its conclusion, of a case toward its possible generalization, of an anecdote toward the lessons one can draw from it, of a conjecture toward the problematic place of its verification—in short, of a point of certainty toward a space of questions. But, by miming the movement of this search "where one becomes lost in delight," the sentence also gives rhythm to the problematic deployment of the concept of space, to its internal difference, which superimposes or intertwines several Mediterraneans.

This multiplicity is different from the one that Braudel himself defines by underscoring the constitutive plurality of Mediterranean space: the geographic plurality of that complex of seas united under the name Mediterranean; the difference between the Mediterranean of the geographers and that of the historians, following all the paths along which human activity, making as well as made by the Mediterranean, is constituted and diffused; the plurality of the temporalities that separate the immobile sea from, or mix it with, traditional activities, the privateering space of merchant ships and the field of great naval battles. The question here doesn't bear on this multiplicity. It bears on the type of unity that gives it meaning. It is then this unity itself that is reduced, that causes the appearance of several ways of uniting the concept of the sea with its lived experience, or its empiricity with its metaphoric function—several symbolic spaces that differently configure the relation between structure and space in which the royal succession is at play, that give a different meaning and power to the very notion of space.

How do we then think about this sea, absent from the royal gaze, and yet called by this gaze to relieve it as a force of history—"the images of light and blue water it has for us"? But it is a resolutely landed sea that Braudel continually invites us to consider: a sea made of liquid plains, of separate basins, where the traffic remains close to the coasts, the traffic itself marked by the small numbers of sailors and fishermen, and even the "great shortage" of the wood needed for shipbuilding.[2] It is a Mediterranean that is constantly effaced between its nearby origin, the mountains that have perhaps made it,[3] and its distant extensions: the deserts of Africa, the steppes of central Asia, the Flemish plains, and the rivers that flow to the Baltic or the North Sea. And doubtless this effacement is in keeping with the aim of the historian, already noticeable in the metaphor that classically identifies the movement of the waves with the disturbance of knowledge. Must we not find "across the troubled waters of time, in spite of the troubled waters,"[4] a starting point, solid ground? Must we not also turn away from the shifting appearances of the sea toward the great regularities of the land that define the functional unity of Mediterranean space? The unity of the Mediterranean, the principle of interiority that makes it a subject of history, is that of a system and network of activities. But how do we think about this network that gives the interior sea its personality? If the sea of history is the one made by men and not by nature alone, beginning with what unifying force, with what dominant activity, do we conceive the human unity of the Mediterranean?

The answer may seem obvious: the activity that unifies a space is that which puts its separate parts into relation with one another—it is exchange. And the organizing pole of this unity is that of the organizing places of this exchange: the urban spaces. Thus the first edition of *The Mediterranean* emphasizes "the obsessive place of the cities in the history of the sea": "Everything leads to them, everything carries the mark of their presence and their force. They command in a sea that is essentially a space of transit. They are and they remain, in the Mediterranean, the real homelands."[5] Convinced by the logic of the demonstration, the reader is surprised in spite of everything that the cities that immediately come to illustrate it, depending on the anecdote or literary reference, are Valladolid, Vicenza, and Viterbo. The choice of these not particularly maritime cities would suffice to indicate that the sea's privileged relation with the city metaphorizes a more fundamental affirmation: the unity of the sea is that of a universe of mercantile circulation.

We know that this affirmation is harshly criticized in the second edition of the work. The alleged primacy of the cities is here placed on the rank of those luminous prestiges that, similar in this regard to the ephemeral rockets of the event, bedazzle the observer who is in too much of a hurry. To this bedazzled vision is opposed a piece of evidence: "the Mediterranean in the sixteenth century was overwhelmingly a world of peasants, of tenant farmers and landowners; crops and harvest were the vital matters of this world and anything else was superstructure, the result of accumulation and of unnatural diversion toward the towns."[6] The heart of Mediterranean activity is no longer the lively movement of exchange but the routines of the peasant universe. Its fundamental rhythm is not that of the productive structures of an economic dynamic; it is that of the spaces of immobility and repetition. But how do we then conceive the unity of these spaces in one space? How do we conceive movement beginning with these juxtaposed immobilities? Braudel, it is true, turns the argument around: specifically, "economic history has to be rethought step by step, starting from these slow, sometimes motionless currents."[7] But this answer puts us at the heart of the problem: how do we understand the privileged tie between this "new" and the universe of permanencies and immobilities, between the new history and the forces that resist the adventure of grand history?

The question of Mediterranean unity may be asked in this way: how do we conceive the relation between the rhythms of history and the conditions of historical intelligibility? The division of history into levels works according to two great criteria of differentiation, the increase in speeds and the complexification of systems of relations. But how do these criteria translate into criteria of intelligibility? What relation is there between the accelerated rationalization of human exchanges and the rationality proper to historical discourse? Seen from close up, the answer to the question is quite ambiguous. The "new economic history" must bring about communication between two schemas of the tripartition of the levels of history that involve two exactly opposite "meanings of history."

The first schema is that of development and progress, and it goes from the simplest activities to the most complex systems of activity and from the lowest to the highest speed. It is the schema that *Capitalism and Material Life* exposes: at the very bottom, the world of repetition, that of the "solutions handed down from time immemorial,"[8] of the narrow enclosure in a circle of almost immutable possibilities; the time of the vanquished, of the "confused inhabitants,"[9] materially and intellectually incapable of leaping to clear the narrow limits of the possible. Higher up, the "lively, garrulous" time of exchanges,[10] on which a third time will be constructed, the time of the victors, of the capitalism that generates a market and a history on the world scale. This movement—of the most backward to the most advanced, from the slowest to the liveliest, from the simplest and most obtuse to the most complex and most rationally organized—is in keeping with the spontaneous teleology of modernity. But it also defines a model of scientific rationality, that according to which the anatomy of man is "the key to the anatomy of the ape." This model of rationality of the great Marxist declarations is also that of the most direct inspirers of the *Annales* revolution. It characterizes the sociology of Halbwachs or the economic history of Simiand. This rationality of social science proposes, in a certain way, to take over defunct royal legitimacy: in place of the sovereign who is incapable of conceiving the Mediterranean, the masters of the great world play of exchanges, cutting across land and sea; in place of the chronicler, the contemporary social scholars of this new mastery—those to whom the study of the complex rationality of contemporary societies and markets gives the intelligence of the less developed forms of activity and relation. We know the importance of this conquering rationality of the king-economist and the scholar-sociologist for the project of the new history. But we also know where its logic, pushed to the extreme, would conduct history: into a subaltern role of explaining residual phenomena.

This siren song of social science is the seduction that history had to resist under the threat of enslavement or death. And it is beginning with this alternative that we must understand the other great tripartite schema, the other "meaning of history" that presides over the definition of the Mediterranean as the *subject* of history and over its being put into writing. The first two stages once again present to us, above the long time of repetitive activities, the time of the mercantile economies and the structures—political, social, and cultural—that give them a place and are transformed with them. But, at the third stage, the relation between the acceleration of the speeds and the growing rationalization is reversed. The sea with the highest speed is the one with the battles and events, those events that "pass across [history's] stage like fireflies," falling back, only just born, like the phosphorescence of the Portuguese shores, into the night that they have illusorily illuminated.[11] In the order of the writing of history, the path from the lowest to the highest speed is that of the intelligibility that gets lost. It doesn't go from the simplest to the most complex, but from the most profound to the most superficial.

The battle of historical rationality is continually fought on two fronts: against the firefly glows of the event and of the chattering of the kings, the ambassadors, or the poor; but also against the conquering rationality of the economic laws and of social science. For the "lively time" of the exchanges that develop and of the societies that are rationalized is also a "garrulous time," a time that talks too much, that hides under the succession of its battles the realities of material life, which were "immensely" important but made "so little noise." We must, then, "reverse the order," that is to say reverse the significance of the meaning according to which this time is traversed: put "in the foreground" those vanquished by mercantile expansion—"the masses themselves, even though they live, as it were, outside the lively, garrulous time of history."[12] The exact accounts that the capitalists and the scholars give of their age are just as deceptive, just as illusorily attached to the "clear and transparent" realities as the chattering of the ambassadors, chroniclers, and pamphleteers. The *economic* measure of the time of the world is again a domestic measure. It must receive its meaning from a geology of time. And, in this geology, the meaning of the traversal by rationality is reversed: it is the most primitive that is the principle of explanation, or rather the matrix of meaning. The lively and garrulous time of history is intelligible only if it is strongly bound to a nearly immobile time, to the spatialized time of the great permanencies. The victors pride themselves on making history. But it is the "vanquished" who give history the ahistorical base without which there is no intelligibility proper to history. The long term, the nearly immobile time of the Mediterranean frozen in its archaism, is not measured for the others in terms of speed. It is much more so the time of historiality, the surface of inscription of the time that makes it possible for there to be a history.

It is therefore through this historial time, through this time of a first geography that a meaning of history is formed. Only the geographization of historical time allows that the battle of long periods and collective phenomena against the chronicling of events and kings does not lead solely to the royalty of the economist or sociologist. Once again it is not a question of the causality of the ground or environment. The space of historiality is first a symbolic space, a surface of inscription of time as productive of meaning. This excess of the symbolic function on all natural determinism is what gives the Braudelian notion of space its singularity, noticeable, in particular, in the chapters devoted to the *physical* unity of the Mediterranean world. We know that the determination of this physical unity requires the recentering of this Mediterranean, which was diffusing toward the deserts of Asia or the ports of Hanse on the inner sea, the Mediterranean *properly speaking*. It is not, then, as the space of circulation or the center of a world of similar contours and paths that the inner sea receives its unity. It is through its climate, through the identical climate that reigns in its heart. From this, it receives the interiority that is lacking in the modern Ocean that has overtaken it with speed: "The ocean too is a human unit and one of the most vigorous of the present day world; it too has been a meeting place and a melting-pot of history. But the Atlantic complex lacks a homogeneous centre comparable to the source of that even light which shines at the heart of the Mediterranean."[13]

A homogeneous center, a world of even light. . . . How does one not feel the excess of these expressions on every empirical description and every scientific determination? Besides, as though simply for the sake of doing so, the analyses and illustrations that follow strive to draw this Mediterranean monochrome toward Nordic grayness: "In October, 1869, Fromentin, leaving Messina by boat, noted, 'grey skies, cold wind, a few drops of rain on the awning. It is sad, it could be the Baltic.' "[14] In the same way as the image makes the light of the inner sea turn to gray, the explanation shows its climatic identity as the outcome of a conflict of exterior forces: the Sahara and the Atlantic, the one spreading toward the north and west to the point of afflicting the coasts of Armorica with dryness; the other repelling it with its rains, shaking the Mediterranean with water to the point of making it resemble "a plain covered with snow."[15] The gap, between the hieratic character of the matrix-formed image (the homogeneous center) and the disparity, the internal difference of the Mediterranean that the description and explanation accentuate into paradoxical images, seems to be systematic: as if the "climatic" unity metaphorized a more fundamental symbolic unity, alone capable of making the inner sea into a subject of history. The monochrome heart or the identical light states, before any geographical explanation, the historiality of the Mediterranean, the "force of history" that succeeds the setting sun of royalty; just as the "creative space"[16] evoked elsewhere, before any consequence of the geographic opening to free economic exchange, is inscribed in the royal vacancy, draws in it the emblematic figure of a death of the king that retains its power of historialization.

The matrix-formed image defines, then, much more than the climatic unity of the Mediterranean. It defines the "sun," the conditions of succession, that make the Mediterranean a subject of history *in place of the king*. It defines the form of legitimacy proper to this passage; this form is not a matter of climatic unity but of the unity of a symbolic space that articulates, on the body of the Mediterranean, figures of discourse as well as perceptible figures. The Mediterranean that succeeds the king must have, as he does, a double body: a body of hidden knowledge and a body of perceptible evidence. The Mediterranean that succeeds the king is the identity of a space of cognition and a space of recognition. From the deceptive glows of the event or the overly transparent realities of exchange, historical science leads us back to the barely perceptible realities that they hide. But these realities, imperceptible for the king of times past or the economist of today, are also those which may be seen, in their identity, by the voyager who traverses the different times that the same Mediterranean space causes to coexist, that "collection of museums of Humanity, of the humanity of another time, but that ever remains the humanity of today":[17] those Arabic boats, in 1897 still similar to the one that Vasco da Gama borrowed; those square-sailed barks that figure on the walls of hypogea and still drift down the Nile, the same "mob of human beings on which the noisiest, the most spectacular invasions turn out to be incapable of biting in depth."[18] If the old illusions of the chronicles and the new illusions of conquering science and capital allow themselves to be reduced in the appropriate measure, it is by the possibility that the voyager of 1930 has of finding the routes of Don Quixote, the people of Bandello or Mateo Alemán. More than the olive tree, what gives the Mediterranean its unity is the possibility of finding the tree, in the same place, such as it was described a long time ago. The Mediterranean is the sea of recognition, of the voyage that passes back over material traces, which the traces of writing show to be similar to themselves.

The unity of the Mediterranean is that of a voyage of return. In the incessant cross-references among the archival document, the geographer's notation, the narrative of the storyteller of yesteryear, and the contemporary impression of a voyage, one senses the fascination for a certain model: that of the voyage on the traces of the book, of the voyage that finds back the places exactly as they were written about. The first edition of *The Mediterranean* clearly shows Braudel's fascination for the unique enterprise of Victor Bérard, who set out to retrace the path of Ulysses to demonstrate his theory: that the Homeric poems are in fact books of geography, and that one can find the land of Calypso, Alcinous, or the lotus-eaters, in a state similar to that found in the Homeric descriptions. Now, we know that photographic *mimesis* takes this recognition into the realm of hallucination by making us *see* the cave of the Cyclops, the willows in the wood of Persephone, the swine of Circe, or the vine of Alcinous. Nonetheless, it is not with its excess but with its lack that Braudel seems to reproach this hallucinatory inquiry: "Victor Bérard sought, for his entire life, the landscapes of the *Odyssey*. A fascinating quest: but is it not the very man of the ancient epic who must be found in the man of today? Ulysses in the flesh, and not only the shifting scenery of his surprising voyages?"[19] Ulysses *in the flesh.* . . . The reference to Victor Bérard will disappear in the second edition, along with the conclusion of the first part, entitled "Geohistory and Determinism." But the conclusion of the book will carry us, following new voyagers, onto the sea of Ulysses that resembles what it was: "Like Audisio and Durrell, I believe that antiquity lives on round today's Mediterranean shores. In Rhodes or Cyprus, 'Ulysses can only be ratified as an historical figure with the help of the fishermen who to-day sit in the smoky tavern of *The Dragon* playing cards and waiting for the wind to change.' "[20] Ulysses ratified: a Ulysses who isn't a liar, a Ulysses of flesh and bone, no longer of paper, whom one may extract from the fiction of Homer like the real Danaë from the poem of Simonides the liar. The historial Mediterranean, the monochrome heart that gives its genuine first principle of unity to the Mediterranean of sailors, merchants, and bankers, is indeed the same sea of writing that bore Danaë and her son intact, the place that takes in and gives passage to meaning by assuring the identity of a *muthos* and a *logos*. The coincidence between the scholarly *geology* of the social times and their geography offered up to view is itself possible because of this coincidence between a material space and a space of writing.

The royal succession, the relieving of the garrulous time of genealogies, chronicles, and prophecies by the space of the inscriptions of material civilization, is possible by reason of that first "mythology" that assures the recovery of a material space and a space of discourse. The Mediterranean is as one neither by climate, exchanges, nor battles; nor by their addition or intertwining. It is as one because it is *such as it was written*. This *such as* brings to life a subject of history by responding to the revisionist challenge of the *no-such*, in which the event of history collapses without redemption or relief. The homogeneous center that makes the Mediterranean beat as the new subject of history is a heart of writing. For the king's force of history to be transmitted to the sea, a historiality or first "geography" must make four places coincide: the Mediterranean space as the world of geographic constraints, the world of exchanges, the empty place of the dead king, and the originary place of all narrative of space, the *Odyssey*. The latter is the book of the written sea, traversed by the text to the point of return, having become, even before the name historian is born, a territory of writing, but also the book that is entirely written on space, through which no heresy, no war of religion, no death by or for the Scripture can occur. It is this identity that the mercantile and conquering Atlantic is lacking, much more than climatic unity. If the great sea of exchanges, which has dethroned the Mediterranean in the government of the world, inherited nothing from the latter's "force of history," it is because no writing covered it in advance. And its writers, late in coming, applied themselves as though to flee it for the African heart of darkness, the confines of Cape Horn, or the enchanted isles of the Pacific. The epic of the Atlantic, *Moby Dick*, is a counter-epic: in place of the sea of the sirens, the Ocean of the Leviathan that fascinates and engulfs, waters that close up, allowing the survival, in the immaculate center of the turbulence, of only the orphan, the cursed child of the Book, Ishmael.

"The Atlantic of Seville is a space without a past," declares Pierre Chaunu, at the threshold of the interpretive part of *Séville et l'Atlantique*.[21] The Atlantic is, in just as decisive a manner, without an *epos* that has written the coincidence of its space with the time of a voyage. In the fashion of the *Odyssey*, the book that makes it exist as an object of history is a catalogue of vessels. And it is quite true that the *libros de registros* of the *Casa de la Contratación* of Seville can easily emblematize, in the face of the mnemonic fancy of the Homeric catalogue, the exemplary material of the new historical science. On the void of all literature, science can construct its virgin space, the space of a "statistical interpretation" of the Atlantic in which nothing figures that is not measurable. But the problem returns: can this exemplary science be written as history? At the end of six volumes of pictures, series, and graphs that integrated into the statistical interpretation the sailing and the tonnage of each of the vessels that entered, over five hundred years, into each port of the new world of Seville, the question is asked: how to write, in the four thousand opening pages, the history of this statistical Atlantic? The most natural way would be to follow the logic of this twofold creation, that of a mercantile space and that of its statistical representation:

> Since nothing is, so to speak, given at the outset in this Atlantic where everything is conjuncture, there is nothing to be inscribed at the outset; rather, each institution, each territory, each way of navigation, exploitation, or exchange is to be situated at the moment in which it appears, in which it is embodied in the progression of time. One would thus have perfectly expressed the truth of the first Atlantic—the truth of a dominant conjuncture that emerges from previously nonexistent structures, more and more important with the constitution of the past of a space that had no past.[22]

The historian nevertheless had to renounce this "paradoxical" solution—that is to say, simply, that it was contrary to the horizon of expectation of nonscholarly vision—for a very simple reason: to accept it was "to condemn oneself to unintelligibility."[23] Beyond all question of "pedagogy," a radical disjunction is stated: following the *logos* according to which an object of history and its scientific interpretation are constituted prohibits writing a book of intelligible history. The historian therefore chooses the "wiser" solution: first exposing the structures—the order of space—before reaching the time of the conjuncture. But the structures in question can in fact structure nothing (one volume will also be missing without missing); they cannot precede any writing, cannot double from any *muthos* the *logos* of Atlantic space. The latter remains a space without historiality. The intelligibility of science and that of narrative have no place to be covered. The *logos* and the *muthos* will remain separate, the book incomplete. The collection of books is doomed to remaining a collection of materials for a book to come. But the open workshop of the scientific future is also the Ocean "where one becomes lost in delight," where the difference between "doing history" and writing history is projected to infinity: the *Odyssey* of research in place of the *Odyssey* of the book; more faithful in a sense to the "ratified Ulysses." For, before bringing him home, the book had, in the voice of Tiresias, condemned him to wander until he arrived in the land of men who had no knowledge of the sea.

A Heretical History?

Between the history of mentalities and that of spaces, the circle of the intelligibility of historical study is completed. There is history—an experience and matter of history—because there is speech in excess, words that cut into life, wars of writing. And there is a historical science because there is something written that quells these wars and scars these wounds by coming back onto the traces of what was already written. There is a history of mentalities because there is heresy and its sanction: bodies marked and tortured for having broken, with an extravagant transversal, the lifeline of the Scripture, the consecrated articulation from the order of speech to the order of bodies: for having denied the "true" relation of the Word to its father and its incarnation, of Adam to his flesh, of the bodies of the resurrected to the bodies of the angels. . . . The heretical separation undoes the "good" attachment of the word to the flesh, of the body to speech. It thereby gives life to erratic speech, "not similar" to what was said. This mortal adventure gives the history of mentalities its matter, and the latter redeems the former in return. To heretical speech, then, the history of mentalities gives another voice, the voice of the place; it gives it a body of immanence, a pagan body. In this way it regulates the war of religion, the war of the Scripture, in a radical manner. It transforms the heretic, the "falsifier" of the Scripture, into a pagan. And a pagan always speaks the truth, for her speech is only the expression of her mode of being. The history of mentalities gives words other flesh, without any subtlety of incarnation, without any hazardous voyage from heaven to earth.

But, for that peaceful regulation that transforms heresy into a mentality to be possible, this pagan flesh—this flesh of land in which speech is rooted—must itself be woven of words. The land that renders a body to the spoken words that have gone astray from the Book of Life is itself prewritten by the words of another book of life, of another idea of the book of life. The romantic revolution in history found this other book of life in the epic conceived as the book of primary expressivity, of the immanence of meaning in the breathing of things. The age of Michelet reinvents the *Odyssey* as the song of the native soil, Victor Bérard finds its traces all around the Mediterranean, and it still offers its prewritten surface to the new history of spaces.

This circle of territorialized speech and written land is foundational, but certainly not because it would give historical science the instruments and methods of its investigation. It gives more and less at the same time: it effectively defines the condition necessary for the product of these instruments and methods to take the form of a history. It gives historical science what even the rigor of calculus or induction would never assure it: a regime of truth for its statements. For history, tied by principle to the disturbance of speech, is forever deprived of the positivist resource that replaces the aporias of the truth with the internal evidence of the rules of construction of experience and of the objects of science. Its *proper* access to science passes through the necessary detour of a *position of the true*. The other social sciences manage, more conveniently, to do without this. They construct the effectiveness of science, to the point of the simulacrum, in such a manner that the plays of well-effected cognition and of "unavoidable" reality exhaust the question of truth. But history can become a science *by remaining history* only through the poetic detour that gives speech a regime of truth. The truth it gives itself is that of a pagan incarnation, of a true body of words substituted for erratic speech. It doesn't give this to itself in the form of an explicit philosophical thesis, but in the very texture of narrative: in the modes of interpretation, but also in the style of the sentences, the tense and person of the verb, the plays of the literal and figurative.

For the "philosophy" to which history is indebted is the one that it does not, at any price, want to hear about, except in the respectable—which is to say denying—form of a reflection on the objects and methods of science. The progression of philosophy since Plato is first of all a wager on the veridicality of a number of narratives—or *muthoi*—taken for *logos*, for imitations or prefigurations of the true. The progression of historical study must itself be founded on such an identity of *muthos* and *logos*. But it must also continually efface it in the involvement of recounted knowledge, and deny it in the gravity of the discourse on the *corpus*—in method and in instrument. It must continually forget that the manner in which it is a science is not that in which it would wish to be.

The mythological regulation of heresy and its scientistic denial of course bear on that disturbance that seizes the new history in the face of its impossible beginning: the democratic disorder of speech born from the void and from abolished royal legitimacy. If the new history found its territory of choice in the long periods of the monarchical, peasant, and Catholic times, it was not by folklorist nostalgia for the times and places of a motionless people. Those times and places alone lend themselves to the operations of meaning that found the intelligibility of the discourse of the new history. It is on this terrain alone that the exchange of voices and bodies can oppose its rigor to the chatter of chronicles—that the force of history of kings can pass to the epic of spaces, and the lost voices of Christian heresy find the pagan body of their interpretation. In the symbolic universe structured by the ordering identities of the royal body, the divine word, and the poetic Muse, the scholarly history of the age of the masses must go searching for its markers. What comes afterward—the history of democratic revolutions, of modern class struggles, of the workers' movement and legend, falls outside its field. The history of the masses that belongs to the age of the masses finds its seat only in speaking of the times of kings. In an apparent paradox, the history of the modern masses seems voluntarily abandoned to the heirs of the old race of chroniclers and hagiographers. "Curiously enough," a specialist writes, "workers' history has remained largely foreign to the renewal of perspectives imposed for more than a quarter of a century by the French school."[1] How do we conceive this foreignness? This is assuredly not a question of methods and instruments. For the historians of long monarchical periods and those of modern social movements have been similarly educated in the economic and statistical school of Simiand and Labrousse. And the latter have over the former the advantage of materials and statistical series that are already partially constituted. It is also not simply that the history of modern social and revolutionary movements is still too near our present, and inspires too many engagements and resentments to enjoy fully the status of scientific object. What much more constitutes its defect are the modes of interpretation and the forms of writing that belong to the regulation of the disturbance of words.

Such a defect is evidently not accidental. It is connected to the very nature of the object. The nature of the modern democratic and social movement is to undo the symbolic order that provides matter for the operations of interpretation and history that belong to the history of mentalities. The historical science of the democratic age can't be the science of its own history. For the distinctive feature of the latter consists in ruining the very ground on which the voices of history let themselves be territorialized. The excess of speech that gives a place to the modern social movement doesn't let itself be *redeemed*. It is true that one can perfectly *reduce* it: industrial mutations and economic cycles, technological changes and urban or factory sociabilities—all of them offer something to bring every excess of speech back to solid determinations. And the diverse variations on the critique of "ideology" provide for the operation without omission. Science is assuredly suited to this, but not history. For the latter needs a poetic regulation of the excess, the substitution of a body of the voice for another—in short, a redemption from the heretical separation. But, at the origin of the modern democratic and social movement, there is a heresy of a new kind: a lay heresy, without religion to torture it, but also without procedures of symbolic redemption.

Revisionist historiography situates this heresy in its own way. It assimilates it to the collapse of a symbolic order and its consequence, the substitutive and terrorist proliferation of the social and democratic imaginary. But to this catastrophic vision, in which history comes to the point of refusing to accept its object, one can oppose the more sober formulas in which democratic and social heresy declares itself by proclaiming a new relation of the order of discourse to the order of bodies. Nothing illustrates this better than the modest event that E. P. Thompson chose as the inaugural scene in the "making" of the English working class: the January 1792 meeting, in a London tavern, of nine honest and industrious workers seized with the singular conviction that every adult person in possession of reason had, as much as anyone else, the capacity to elect the members of Parliament. The medium they chose for the diffusion of this idea was a "Corresponding Society." And the first rule decreed for this society and for every similar society to use was stated as follows: "That the number of our Members be unlimited."[2]

Nothing here seems out of the ordinary. And nonetheless it is heresy, the "separation" constitutive of the modern social movement, that is declared. The rupture of the symbolic markers in the political order is at work in the constitution of this hitherto unknown subject of speech that is defined in the relation of three propositions. First, one man counts as much as another; the order of speakers is exclusive of all exclusion. Second, the political subject that sets itself to the task of verifying this proposition bears the mark of the unlimited. It can't be numbered because it is the pure denial of exclusion. Third, the mode of speech and contact that suits this new mode of political subjectification is correspondence, pure address to everyone else without belonging or subjection that establishes the community of the present and the absent. The modern social movement has its place of origin in this pure rupture or pure opening, which the political practices of incorporation and the modes of objectification of social science will apply themselves to warding off: it is that of a class that is no longer a class but "the dissolution of all classes." This formula, as we know, is from the young Marx. But it is possible to renew its meaning by removing it from the images of decomposition that he associates with it. The class that declares itself in the pure invocation of its limitlessness of number is rather identified with the act of a speech without place and of an uncountable collectivity, one impossible to identify. It is the advent, in the field of politics, of a subject that is such only in its recrossing and disjunction of the modes of legitimacy that established the affinity between discourses and bodies.

The democratic and social age is then neither the age of the masses nor that of individuals. It is the age of hazardous subjectification, engendered by a pure opening of the unlimited, and constituted from places of speech that are not designatable localities but rather singular articulations between the order of speech and that of classifications. Thus the places of speech from which the limitlessness of the working "class" is projected are not factories or barracks, streets or cabarets. They are texts, phrases, names: reference texts—the Rights of Man or the Old Testament—that permit the articulation of an experience otherwise kept in silence by the separation of languages; phrases and arrangements of phrases that transform, into something visible and utterable, what had no place to be distinguished and was heard only as inarticulate noise, moving into common space new subjects, new legitimacies, and forms in which the former can argue from the latter; words, removed from the common language of designations—names of classes that do not designate any specific collection of individuals but the very disruption of the relations between names and states of affairs. Such is the name of proletarian reclaimed by Blanqui in the face of the judge who asks him his profession and becomes indignant with the response: for *proletarian* is not a profession as he understands it, that is to say a trade; it is a profession in a much older and entirely new sense, a declaration of belonging to the community that specifically counts the uncounted. These names of classes that are not classes are themselves tied to names of actions that answer no protocol and no definite apprenticeship (emancipation), but adjust the unlimited space of new paths by making subjects of speech and history travel in the hazardous intervals between material places and symbolic places, between names and bodies, conditions and knowledge.

The heresy that is inherent in democratic and social historicity must thus be conceived according to a twofold scheme. It is first situated empirically, in the profusion of deviating religions and heterodox forms of knowledge that provoked and accompanied the emergence of the modern social movements. E. P. Thompson showed quite well how the industrial revolution, working conditions, and the traditions of the trades were by themselves powerless to bring on the birth of a working class and movement in England. It was necessary for their experience to be caught in the web of a war of writing in which the new Declaration of the Rights of Man, intersecting with the biblical prophecies and the injunctions of *Pilgrim's Progress*, came to mobilize anew and divide along new lines the energies of religious dissidence. It is, or at least it should be, equally impossible to think about the French history of the workers' movement outside the network of connections that bring its subject into existence at the intersections of the new religions of industry or love, the pedagogical revolutions and elaborations of self-education, the extravagant philologies and the new languages, the heterodox medical practices and knowledge, popular astronomy and the speculations about distant, past, and future worlds. But this empirical dispersion obeys a more essential logic. The capture of the worker-subject in the extravagant paths of heretical knowledge and belief do not mark the mere influence of the ideas of a time on the first formulations of a movement still in its infancy. It actualizes the singular mode of being of the subjects of history in the democratic age. The latter are neither the proper names of sovereigns whose bodies and speech would govern a world of hierarchized orders, nor the common names of classes that science would define by the coherence of their properties. They are the singular names, falsely proper and falsely common, of a being-together without place or body—of a being-together that is a being-between: between several places and several identities, several modes of localization and identification. This heresy or modern errancy has, then, an unheard-of property: it is identical to the very principle of the law that, by declaring the rights of man *and* of the citizen, installs the democratic subject in the infinite of their separation and their reciprocal contestation, and in the same motion puts its history outside the assurances of subordination, into the uncertainties of conjunction.

This division, in its very principle, of the democratic subject "itself" is what the Micheletist revolution could regulate only in the form of compromise. Its intention was to suture the division of democracy by reconciling it with its past. It found the means of warding off the *explicit* violence of the democratic advent, the regicidal rupture. Beyond the violence of the revolutionary confrontation, it invented a logic of sense, a way of thinking about the twofold filiation, reattaching the Republic of Law to its land-matrix. The logic of the place of speech sealed the threefold—scientific, narrative, and political—contract. By tying the chattering voices of *mimesis* into the narrative of silent meaning, it effects a twofold operation: it rooted the modern Republic in its history and in its territory; it opened a democratic interpretation of the history of monarchical and inquisitorial times, an interpretation in terms of the history of the masses and of long periods. It gave a common place to the politics of the sovereign people and to scholarly history. And it could do this because it was, in its own way, a logic of the subject, the subject named *France*. The compromise stemmed from this incarnation that fixed the erratic properties of democratic subjectivity into the attributes of a subject identical to itself. In this regard, the history of the *Annales* school is that of an emancipation or a forgetting— progressive and thwarted—with respect to the subjective and political conditions of the compromise: the subject of history became an object, or rather a place, among other places, for objects of history; the long period was detached from filiation and advent; the logic of the place of speech was set in an ethnohistory. Thus the democratic interpretation of monarchical and inquisitorial times could be emancipated into the history of mentalities, while the historian became the child of no one, the mere sibling of all the laborers enlisted in the workplace of science.

We can say, then, that the apparent paradox that removes the "new" history from its own time is the price of this forgetting. Set to the task of redeeming regicidal violence and heretical separation, scholarly history forgot the meaning and conditions of this redemption. It simply assimilated them to the scientific promotion of historical discourse. It thereby rendered itself incapable of renewing the contract. And the successes of the history of spaces, long periods, and mentalities had, on the other hand, forced the incapacity of thinking the "other side" of the royal death, its diffuse symbolic violence: the dispersion of the attributes of sovereignty into the hazards of democratic subjectification and the loops of social heresy. But we can also say that the Micheletist contract was itself an unstable compromise, a desperate will to lock the democratic rupture in the becoming-republican of the subject *France*. It thereby made history into the narrative of an advent, the history of a prehistory, called to abolish itself in the time without history of a just republic. Giving the republican age the means of thinking and writing its prehistory, the contract prohibited it, in the same gesture, from conceiving its own history and the forms of its writing. It freed the republican age from democratic heresy. The latter, in return, was devoted, by the very development of its characteristics, to indefinitely deregulating the poetic formulas of the scientific redemption of heresy.

The difficulty that places the social history of the democratic and workers' age on the margins of the great history of mentalities is therefore not where we willingly put it: in the battle of causes, in the opposition between the healthy materialism of economic and sociological determinations and the pretension of ideological causes. To conceive the heretical nature of the modern social movement is not to rehabilitate the role of "ideas" and "consciousness." What determines the life of speakers, as much as and more than the weight of labor and of its remuneration, is that of spoken and written—read and heard—names, a weight that is just as material as the other one. The question therefore doesn't concern the correct order of causes. It concerns the regime of truth that ties historical discourse to its object. Democratic and social heresy were denounced a thousand times as a "new religion." But this "religion" can't be territorialized and converted as the other one can. The excess of words can therein be mastered only at the risk of canceling the force and meaning of history attached to their enunciation. For the social history of the democratic and workers' age quickly falls into a dilemma: either it is reduced to the chronicling of proper names that no longer organize any legitimacy of discourse or any meaning of history—monographs on a combat or a militant, on a party, a union, or a newspaper; or it is the science that restores these surface individualities and agitations to their foundation, by determining the subterranean realities of which they are the local and punctual expression. But, between the proper names of chronicling and the common names of science, it is the very material and discourse of history that once again run the risk of vanishing: its material, which is to say the speech event, the path along which speakers devote themselves to the truth of their speech; its discourse, which is to say the reinscription of this event in the equivalence of narrative and science.

It is true that social history sometimes believes it has found the means to get out of the dilemma, to fill in the gap between the rigor of economic and social determinations and the event-based character of manifestations and discourses. For the excess of democratic and social speech, it believes it has found a place. The latter is called *culture* or *sociabilities*. These concepts refer the excess of words to the expression of modes of being and ways of doing. But the book, the earth, and the tomb are lacking in the territorialization and redemption of this excess. Besides, it is then possible to assign this excess a residence. "Popular sociabilities" or "workers' culture" come to fill the imaginary gap between material life and the speech event. And, in the same motion, they come to fill the intervals in democratic (republican, socialist, worker . . .) being-together that settle among several places and several identities. What they propose to explain, they simply make disappear. This is attested exemplarily by these explanations of workers' speech that assign it, since it has no earth or sea to take it in, to the culture of trade, and make it, indifferently, into the expression of its proud qualification or painful disqualification. Words, whatever the realists might say, are more stubborn than facts, and *trade*, as soon as it is invoked and argued in the social conflict, allows the bond to speak, the bond that keeps it attached to servitude or the splendor of the *minister*, as *profession* to the glory of a *declaration* or the shame of an *avowal*. The name *proletarian* is explicit about its Latin etymology (the multitude given to simple reproduction) much more than the "rigorous" definitions over which historians and sociologists wear themselves out. Whatever one might argue about the greatness and decadence of the various trades, a mechanic, when he becomes a social combatant, is first a man of iron, a typographer a man of the letter, and a tailor a man of appearance. And, if the shoemakers were the first to raise, practically everywhere, the curtain of the workers' movement, the successes and failures of the shoe industry had nothing to do with it; all that mattered was the fact that shoemakers have been, from the earliest ages, the most named, spoken of, and above all cursed workers, in profane and sacred writing.

The identity of social combatant is thus not the expression of the "culture" of some group or subgroup. It is the invention of a name for the picking up of several speech-acts that affirm or challenge a symbolic configuration of relations between the order of discourse and the order of states of affairs. It is first the denial of an exclusion set by another's speech when, for example, the modern strike declares itself to be "under a government which pretends that we are not human like the others."[3] It is also the identification of the one designated as excluded when public space resounds with the call to the "wretched of the earth," or with the affirmation that "we are all German Jews." It is finally the opening of the space and time in which those who do not count are counted, when the organization assumes its tasks: "You are wrestling with the Enemies of the human Race . . . for the Child hanging at the Breast."[4] The three formulas—denial, identification, and opening—equally affirm the essential trait of the declaration of a social subject: this declaration is a *heterology*, a logic of the other, a position between words and things. It is unthinkable in terms of the consciousness—even a confused one—of a proper identity, utterable only from the point of view of another, in the play of three figures: the master who assigned names to places; the new identity woven of names borrowed from and taken out of language; the absolute alterity of the excluded, who may be the wretched but also the *infans*, the one who doesn't speak yet. The concept of culture, whether one applies it to knowledge of the classics or the manufacture of shoes, has the sole effect of effacing this movement of subjectification that operates in the interval between several nominations and its constitutive fragility: the absence of the body instead of the voice, the absence of the voice instead of the body, the rift or the interval through which subjects of history pass. It identifies and localizes what has its being only in the gap of places and identities.

Cultural history is therefore just as powerless to tell us the reasons for some figure or other of social combat as the "contemporary sociologist" is to tell us what "in truth" were the social classes and their relations in the French Revolution. The truth is not the affair of auxiliaries. No more than it can defer to some sister or auxiliary science can history discard its question onto one of its supposed provinces or subdivisions. Social history and cultural history are not sectors of history available for a brotherly touch. These are two names for the same question: that of the procedures of meaning by which a historicity is defined—that is to say the possibility that subjects in general would make a history—and of the forms of writing that account for them by inscribing them in the genre of a narrative and the figure of a truth. The problem with our historical science is first that of a necessary and unhappy relation with "its" historicity, democratic historicity: the dispersion of the attributes of sovereignty and of the various logics of subordination, the undefined difference between the man and the citizen, the possibility for any speaker or any aleatory collection of speakers to be in any way subjects of history. The logic of filiation and the procedures of territorialization of meaning that belong to romantic republican history lose their power in this relation. The historian then easily comes out of it to despair quite plainly of the possibility of holding narrative and truth together. On every possible figure of narrative, she sees the dilemma arise: either narrative and its kindness toward chance heroes, or science dissipating their prestige; either the great popular epic that is like a dream in its telling, or the disenchanted rigors of number or even the discouraging minutiae of real, everyday and domestic, life. She settles within the logic of a suspicion, voluntarily or not: for the subjects and events of democratic and social historicity, always too close to our sentiments and angers, marked too much by the stigmata of "ideology," it seems that the truth wins only through a growth in scientific guarantees or in scientistic redemption. This increase, of course, is never sufficient. But the very play of its deception in return produces an increased difficulty with regard to the "subject" and a renewed suspicion with regard to narrative—even if this suspicion comes back with the accusation of scholarly insufficiency, on the point of political rigor. If Marxism did so little for the history of "its" age, if historical science also specialized in the history of its own pre-history—the agrarian crises, the advent of the market, and the mentalities of monarchical times—it was by the necessity of the circular logic in which the political suspicion concerning the discourse of history responds to the scientific suspicion concerning the subject of history. That is why the proclaimed lapsing of Marxism does not itself open any new path. The two forms of the suspicion could come together only to deter the history of the democratic and workers' times from attempting on its own account what the republican romantic revolution had done, and from which the history of mentalities had benefited: a poetic operation on the conditions of knowledge.

The history of mentalities lived on the antiliterary literary work of Michelet: the invention of a narrative of immanence of meaning in narrative, of a narrative that suppressed heretical extravagance by the latter's own routes. Thanks to this invention, the history of mentalities was able to territorialize the lost voices of heresy and the insignificant paths of poor life onto the two great books of life, the Christian book of the word made flesh and the pagan book of the written earth. The unthinkable extravagance that social and workers' history, with perhaps two or three exceptions, prohibited itself from imagining—and that was nonetheless strictly necessary to it—was simply finding, for itself, a poetics. And without doubt, to find it, one had to go a little bit ahead, on the side of the literary revolution: where the novel says good-bye to the epic, where the parataxis of democratic coordinations succeeds the syntax of monarchical subordinations, where notice is taken of the defection of the great books of life, as well as of the multiplicity of both languages and modes of subjectification. To get out of the desperate dilemma between the illusion of the popular *epos* and the rigors of number or the minutiae of the everyday, one had to attach oneself to the new logics invented by literature to hold together the paths of the individual and the law of number, the little glimmers of the everyday and the flame of the sacred texts. One had to learn how to give birth to narrative from, for example, Virginia Woolf—"between the acts," from the promise of a sentence that has emerged from the same silence as the subjects of the democratic age and their waiting for tomorrow (" 'Yes, of course, if it's fine tomorrow,' said Mrs. Ramsay. 'But you'll have to be up with the lark,' she added").[5] Or to see how, in Flaubert, from the non-sense of a distorted name (Charbovari) the history of mutilated lives comes out. Or to follow, in Joyce, the peregrinations of the new Ulysses, insular, urban, and deceived by his spouse, turning in a circle in his colonized people's city, torn apart by the multiplicity of languages, putting to ill use, the one by way of the other, the Christian book of life and the pagan book of life. Or even to accompany Claude Simon in his "attempt at reinstating a baroque altar" in which the explosion of the ordered syntax of the narrative—this "filler cement" or this "sticky sauce" capable of putting together meaning from any ruins—and the claimed independence of the life that finds back, in the disarticulated phrase, its profusion without beginning or end are associated with the vision of an anti-Mediterranean: sea-earth or mother of writing, henceforth weary of serving as a "sewer" or "gutter" for history.[6]

Without doubt several excursions of this kind were necessary for the democratic and workers' age to size up its subject and invent the forms of writing suited to formulate its subject's suspended truth. But, in the tension between the assurance of the rules of knowledge and the hazard of the blows of the truth, each science has the tendency to bet in inverse proportion to its own assurance. And the suspicion weighing on so-called contemporary history has too easily pushed it to hang on to the arms and insignias of scientificity, rather than seek to draw the figure of the historicity that belongs to its age. The opposition of serious science and literature quite naturally offers to transform this retreat into a virtue. What the reassuring proscription of "literature" seeks to ward off is simply this: by refusing to be reduced to the mere language of numbers and graphs, history agreed to tie the fate of its demonstrations to that of the procedures by which common language produces meaning and causes it to circulate. Demonstrating, in the common language, that the documents and curves compose a meaning, and *such* a meaning, will always assume a choice with regard to powers of language and of its linkings. There is no assemblage of words to the effect of monstration or demonstration that doesn't effect such a choice, that doesn't produce, in this sense, "literature." The problem is therefore not to know if the historian does or doesn't have to produce literature, but what literature he produces. In practice the historian knows very well, like the sociologist, how to interrupt the analysis of the statistical results discreetly, in order to insert the little narrative that gives it, in one stroke, flesh and meaning—the teacher's notebook, the memory of some childhood, the rustic or working-class novel. But this shameful poetics of itself immediately denies what it effects, the substitution of one language and one procedure of meaning for another. It transforms the little narrative into a little window, for a time open to what the numbers say in "their" language. It makes it into the fragment of an improbable literature, similar to that which the schoolbooks of the past cut up, to represent with mirrors the table of language and the table of things. If it still mimes the Micheletist procedures of the territorialization of meaning, it does so furtively, sufficiently sensing that this manner is no longer of the time that it must think about, but in the same gesture ceasing, in most cases, to think about it.

The question of the poetic form according to which history can be written is then strictly tied to that of the mode of historicity according to which its objects are thinkable. Michelet invented a poetics for a certain historicity, for the genealogy of the subject France and of the form Republic. Frightened with such an invention, contemporary history can only prohibit itself from thinking about the very forms of the historicity with which it is confronted: the forms of the sensory experience, of the perception of time, of the relations of belief and knowledge, of the near and the distant, of the possible and the impossible that have constituted the democratic and social age as the age of the wait, the age governed by the empire of the future; the forms of the experience of the name and anonymity, of the proper and the common, of the image and the identification that have oriented this wait toward both the imagination of the community and the discovery of individuality. It is assuredly a strange paradox that the history of mentalities ceases to be interested in the feeling of time precisely when time goes mad, where the future becomes an essential dimension of individual and collective action; that it ceases to be interested in belief when the latter enters into the immanence of political and social action, while there is a disruption of the relations between the present and the nonpresent, the visible and the nonvisible, which mark the perceptible indicators of its territory. This lack of interest, which opposes the good ways of *writing history* to the vain illusions of a time in which one thought oneself to be *writing history*, in fact leads to a well-determined limit: the sacrifice of history itself to the affirmation of scientistic belief. This sacrifice can take the gentle form of a vanishing of history into social or political science. It can also take the form of the declared closure of its object. The "end of history" is thereby posted in our orders of the day. What we commonly designate by this expression is the end of a certain historicity, the sealed interval of democratic and social heresy, of two centuries of bad or false history, giving way to an industrial and liberal modernity finally delivered to the harmonious development of its nature. But one also designates by it the end of the belief in history as a figure of rationality.

This end of belief can itself take two forms. It sometimes takes that of a placement of history in penitence, in the shadow of the more knowledgeable or wiser sciences. It also takes that of the great encyclopedic workshops, open-closed on the interminable toil of their enrichment and rectification: history unbound from the peril of its homonymy but perhaps reduced in the end to tasks of recapitulation and transmission. Walter Benjamin recently accused the science of history of devoting itself, in its very theory, to continually delivering the past to the victors. Certainly, the present circumstances are in no way comparable to those that provoked the desperate accents of his "Theses on the Philosophy of History." But the shameless inanity with which today one proclaims the opening of a time that is henceforth without history and delivered solely to the performance of the "winners" clearly allows an alternative to appear: Either history first puts itself to consolidating its "scientific" recognition, at the risk of liquidating its particular adventure, by furnishing the society of the victors with the encyclopedia of its prehistory. Or it first gets interested in the exploration of the multiple paths at the unforeseen intersections by which one may apprehend the forms of experience of the visible and the utterable, which constitute the uniqueness of the democratic age and also allow the rethinking of other ages. It becomes interested in the forms of writing that render it intelligible in the interlacing of its times, in the combination of numbers and images, of words and emblems. To do this it consents to its own fragility, to the power it holds from its shameful kinship with the makers of histories and the tellers of stories. A historian recently deplored the "crisis of self-confidence" introduced into his discipline by the rumors and parasitic turmoils of "adjacent disciplines" that wish to submit it to the evil empire of the text and its deconstruction, to the fatal lack of distinction between the real and the imaginary.[7] We will conclude the opposite: nothing threatens history except its own lassitude with regard to the time that has made it or its fear before that which makes its material sensitive to its object—time, words, and death. History doesn't have to protect itself from any foreign invasion. It only needs to reconcile itself with its own name.

Notes

A Secular Battle

1. [The author is invoking the homonymy in the French word *histoire*, which means both story and history.—Trans.]

2. Fernand Braudel, *La Méditerranée et le monde méditerranéen à l'époque de Philippe II* (Paris: Armand Colin, 1949), 184.

[Most of Rancière's references to Braudel's *magnum opus* are to this edition; in the case of modifications, he refers to the second edition. Wherever possible, my references are to the English edition, a translation of the second edition. Where it is not possible—as in this citation—I translate from the first edition.

[In the case of all of Rancière's citations, if there is an English edition available, I refer to it; if not, I provide a translation of the French.—Trans.]

3. Louis Bourdeau, *L'Histoire et les historiens* (Paris: Félix Alcan, 1888), 120.

4. Ibid.

5. Ibid., 122.

6. Ibid.

7. Ibid., 29.

8. Ibid., 291–92.

The Dead King

1. Fernand Braudel, *The Mediterranean and the Mediterranean World in the Age of Philip II*, trans. Siân Reynolds (New York: Harper & Row, 1973), 2:1234. [Translation slightly modified.]

2. Ibid., 1236.

3. Ibid.

4. Paul Ricoeur, *Time and Narrative*, trans. Kathleen McLaughlin and David Pellauer (Chicago: University of Chicago Press, 1984). It goes without saying that this dissociation is by no means a negligence but rather depends on the phenomenological perspective of the author.

5. Emile Benveniste, *Problems in General Linguistics*, trans. Mary Elizabeth Meek (Coral Gables, Fla.: University of Miami Press, 1971), 195–215.

6. Fernand Braudel, *Capitalism and Material Life 1400–1800*, trans. Miriam Kochan (London: Weidenfeld and Nicolson, 1973), p. 45. [Translation slightly modified. The emphasis is Rancière's.—Trans.]

7. Braudel, *The Mediterranean*, 1:21.

8. Thomas Hobbes, *Leviathan*, ed. Richard Tuck (Cambridge: Cambridge University Press, 1991), 225–28; *De Cive or The Citizen*, ed. Sterling P. Lumprecht (New York: Appleton-Century-Crofts, 1949), 128–40.

The Excess of Words

1. Tacitus, *Annals*, bk. 1, chap. 16, in *The Works of Tacitus*, the Oxford Translation (London: Bell, 1888); quoted in Erich Auerbach, *Mimesis*, trans. Willard R. Trask (Princeton: Princeton University Press, 1968), 35.

2. Tacitus, quoted in Auerbach, 36.

3. I would like to refer, on this subject, to my book *Le philosophe et ses pauvres* (Paris: Fayard, 1983), 135–55.

4. Alfred Cobban, *The Social Interpretation of the French Revolution* (Cambridge: Cambridge University Press, 1968), 33.

5. Ibid., 21.

6. Cf. Jean-Claude Milner, *Les Noms indistincts* (Paris: Le Seuil, 1983), and particularly chap. 11, "Les classes paradoxales."

7. Cobban, *The Social Interpretation*, 22.

8. François Furet, *Interpreting the French Revolution*, trans. Elborg Forster (Cambridge: Cambridge University Press, 1981), 22. [Translation slightly modified.]

9. Ibid., 22.

10. Ibid., 24.

11. Ibid., 25.

12. Ibid., 28.

13. Ibid., 25.

14. Ibid., 24.

15. Ibid., 72.

16. Ibid., 73.

The Founding Narrative

1. As we can see, the semiologist Roland Barthes carried this out masterfully in his *Michelet*, trans. Richard Howard (Oxford: Basil Blackwell, 1987). Any reflection on the poetics of knowledge, whatever its perspective may be, is indebted to this book, as it is to several other important texts by the same author.

2. Jules Michelet, *History of the French Revolution*, trans. Charles Cocks (Chicago: University of Chicago Press, 1967), 440–41. [Translation slightly modified. Most references will be to this edition; but since it comprises only the first part of Michelet's work, an occasional reference to Keith Botsford's translation of subsequent portions will be necessary.—Trans.]

3. Lucien Febvre, "Parole, matière première de l'histoire," in *Annales d'histoire sociales* 15 (1943), 91.

4. Michelet, *History of the French Revolution*, 442–43.

5. Ibid., 443.

6. Ibid.

7. Ibid.

8. Ibid., 446.

9. Ibid., 441.

10. Michelet, *History of the French Revolution: Histoire de la révolution française*, trans. Keith Botsford (Wynnewood, Pa.: Livingston, 1973), 6:156. [Translation slightly modified.]

11. Michelet, *History of the French Revolution* (Cocks translation), 448.

12. Ibid., 445–46.

13. Ibid., 445.

14. Ibid., 444; emphasis added.

15. Ibid., 445.

16. Ibid., 447.

17. Ibid.

18. Ibid., 448.

19. Ibid., 451.

20. I refer, on this point, to Philippe Lacoue-Labarthe and Jean-Luc Nancy, *The Literary Absolute*, trans. Philip Bernard and Cheryl Lester (Albany, N.Y.: SUNY Press, 1988).

21. Jules Michelet, *Oeuvres complètes* (Paris: Flammarion, 1973), 3:607.

22. If Michelet speaks of the ocean and not the sea, it is not out of deference to the old Hesiodic divinity. It is in his own "mythology" that the Ocean takes on a determined significance. The Ocean is the sea insofar as the latter has a voice. "Ocean is a voice. . . . As it is the prolific crucible wherein creation began and wherein it is continued, in all its potency, it possesses a living language; it is life speaking to life." *The Sea*, trans. W. H. Davenport Adams (London: T. Nelson and Sons, 1875), 300.

23. [The word "signifiance" simply translates the French *signifiance*. This word has

come to refer to the capacity of elements of language, in different combinations, to produce meaning — meaning that will be different, and will become excessive, when the same set of elements (a phrase or sentence, for example) moves from context to context — and thereby to engage the speaking subject, entering into a determined system of language, in the process of production. — Trans.]

24. Giambattista Vico, *The New Science of Giambattista Vico*, trans. Thomas Goddard Bergin and Max Harold Fisch (Ithaca, N.Y.: Cornell University Press, 1968), 150.

25. Michelet, *Oeuvres complètes*, 3:610.

26. Ibid.; emphasis added.

The Place of Speech

1. Jules Michelet, *Mother Death: The Journal of Jules Michelet, 1815–1850*, trans. and ed. Edward K. Kaplan (Amherst: University of Massachusetts Press, 1984), 121–22.

2. Ibid., 122–23. At issue is the last line of *Oedipus at Colonus*.

3. Jules Michelet, preface to the 1869 edition of the *Histoire de France*, in *Le Moyen Age* (Paris: Robert Laffont, 1981).

4. "The condition for understanding a social fact is that one represent to oneself the man or group of men who are its author; and that one be able to link it to a psychological state, very vaguely defined, perhaps, but sufficiently known to allow us to understand it — the motive for the act." Charles Seignobos, *La Méthode historique appliquée aux sciences sociales* (Paris: F. Alcan, 1901), 215.

5. Michel de Certeau, *The Mystic Fable*, trans. Michael B. Smith (Chicago: University of Chicago Press, 1992), 1:271.

6. Ibid., 39.

7. Jules Michelet, *Satanism and Witchcraft: A Study in Medieval Superstition*, trans. A. R. Allinson (New York: Citadel Press, 1939), xiv.

8. Braudel, *The Mediterranean*, 1:38.

9. Ibid., 2:807.

10. Ibid., 825.

11. Ibid., 1:415–16.

12. Emmanuel Le Roy Ladurie, *Montaillou, village occitan de 1294 à 1394* (Paris: Gallimard, 1975), 524–25. [Barbara Bray's translation of this book, *Montaillou: Cathars and Catholics in a French Village, 1294–1324* (London: Scolar Press, 1978), a shorter version of the French, doesn't include the passages that Rancière here quotes. — Trans.]

13. Ibid., 526.

14. Ibid., 541.

15. Ibid., 9.

16. Ibid., 541.

17. Ibid., 345.

The Space of the Book

1. Braudel, *The Mediterranean*, 2:1236–37.
2. Braudel, *La Méditerranée*, 300.
3. Braudel, *The Mediterranean*, 1:51–52.
4. Braudel, *La Méditerranée*, 246.
5. Ibid., 292.
6. Braudel, *The Mediterranean*, 2:1241.
7. Ibid., 1:241–42.
8. Braudel, *Capitalism and Material Life*, xii.
9. Ibid., xi.
10. Ibid., xv.
11. Braudel, *The Mediterranean*, 2:901.
12. Braudel, *Capitalism and Material Life*, xv.
13. Braudel, *The Mediterranean*, 1:231.
14. Ibid., 232.
15. Ibid., 233.
16. Ibid., 2:1239.
17. Braudel, *La Méditerranée*, 298.
18. Ibid.
19. Ibid., 299.
20. Braudel, *The Mediterranean*, 2:1239.
21. Pierre Chaunu, *Séville et l'Atlantique* (Paris: Armand Colin, 1959), v. 8, 8.
22. Ibid., 11–12.
23. Ibid., 12.

A Heretical History?

1. Yves Lequin, *Les Ouvriers de la région lyonnaise dans la seconde moitié du XIXe siècle (1848–1914)* (Lyon: Presses Universitaires de Lyon, 1977), v.

2. E. P. Thompson, *The Making of the English Working Class* (London: Penguin, 1980), 19.

3. Grignon, *Réflexions d'un ouvrier tailleur . . .* (Paris, 1833), in Alain Faure and Jacques Rancière, *La Parole ouvrière* (Paris: Union Générale d'Editions, 1976), 74.

4. Instructions of the London Corresponding Society to its traveling delegates, 1796; quoted in E. P. Thompson, 16.

5. Virginia Woolf, *To the Lighthouse* (San Diego: Harcourt Brace Jovanovich, 1990), 3.

6. Claude Simon, *The Wind*, trans. Richard Howard (New York: George Braziller, 1959), 144.

7. Lawrence Stone, "History and Postmodernism," *Past and Present* 131 (1991): 217–18. See also, in 133 (1991): 204–209, Patrick Joyce's response.

Index

Compiled by Hassan Melehy

111

Jacques Rancière is currently professor of aesthetics in the Department of Philosophy at the University of Paris-VII (Jussieu). Rancière is the author of numerous books, the most recent of which is *Courts Voyages au pays du peuple* (1990), and has published extensively on problems of ideology, language-events, social history, and historiography in general. Two of his books have appeared in English: *The Nights of Labor: The Worker's Dream in Nineteenth-Century France* (1989) and *The Ignorant Schoolmaster: Five Lessons in Intellectual Emancipation* (1991).

Hassan Melehy holds a Ph.D. in comparative literature and currently teaches in the Department of French and Italian at Miami University. He conducts research in early modern French, philosophy, cultural theory, and cinema, and is continually searching for ways to extend interdisciplinarity.

Hayden White is professor of historical studies at the University of California, Santa Cruz, where he teaches in the History of Consciousness Program. He is author of a number of books on the writing of history, literary theory, and the philosophy of history. His best-known book is *Metahistory* (1973).